INSIGHT POCKET GUIDE

Tallinn

£1

D0353916

Discover
CHANNEL

APA PUBLICATIONS
Part of the Langenscheidt Publishing Group
L

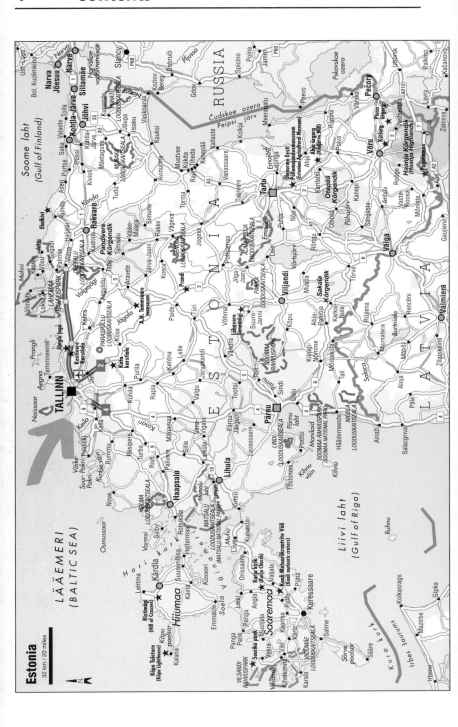

Welcome

This is one of 133 itinerary-based *Pocket Guides* produced by the editors of Insight Guides, whose books have set the standard for visual travel guides since 1970. With top-quality photography and authoritative recommendations, this guidebook is designed to help visitors get the most out of Tallinn and its surroundings during a short stay. To this end, Steven Q. Roman, Insight's expert on Estonia, has devised 14 easy-to-follow itineraries linking the essential sights and exploring some hidden gems.

The first three routes cover the Old Town's major sights and museums, while tour 4 focuses on Tallinn's leafy park area, Kadriorg. The rest of the city itineraries explore Tallinn's other historical sites and intriguing outlying areas. The last four tours suggest excursions beyond the city and include a visit to Helsinki, the vibrant Finnish capital; Haapsalu, a peaceful seaside resort; Naissaar, once a highly restricted military base and now a nature reserve; and the coastal Lahemaa National Park. There are, in addition, sections on history and culture, eating out, shopping and nightlife, plus a calendar of special events. A detailed practical information section towards the end of the guide covers transport, money matters, communications, etc, and includes reviews of hotels and accommodation options in all price categories.

 Steve Roman, a freelance journalist and travel writer, first visited Tallinn as a student in Soviet times, and was so impressed by the city's fairytale charm that he 'accidentally' missed his flight to Leningrad just to stay an extra day. Since moving to Tallinn from Moscow in 1997, the San Francisco native has become an expert on the local dining and nightlife scene, and currently works as a regular contributor to *The Baltic Times* weekly and the *Tallinn In Your Pocket* city guide. On most weekend evenings you can find him haunting the city's trendier lounges and clubs.

6   contents

HISTORY AND CULTURE

From Tallinn's founding to the city's emergence as a tourist hotspot in the late 20th century – a concise introduction to the history of the Estonian capital. **11**

CITY ITINERARIES

These 10 itineraries, which can last from a few hours to a full day, cover the historic city centre and other main attractions in and around Tallinn.

Preceding Pages: view over Town Hall Square
Following Pages: St Catherine's Passage in the snow

History & Culture

On certain streets, in a certain light, it's easy to forget that Tallinn is the capital of a modern, European nation. The illusion is especially powerful in the Old Town, which developed from the 13th to 16th centuries and, at first glance, seems to be an architectural showpiece left over from the city's economic heyday. Scratch the surface, however, and you'll see a patchwork of architectural styles – clues to the bigger story of Estonia and its people, which is one of repeated invasion and conquest by stronger regional powers.

Being a small nation sandwiched between various empires has spelt trouble for the Estonians. For most of the past eight centuries, they have been forced to bow to a succession of foreign masters – Danes, Germans, Swedes, Russians and, more recently, Nazis and Soviets. It's only due to their stubborn character and fiercely independent spirit that the Estonians have managed to survive through the years with their language and culture intact.

King of the Hill

Not much is known about life in Estonia before the first conquerors, the Danes, arrived in 1219. The natives were a Finno-Ugric people (ancient cousins of the Finns), whose ancestors are thought to have migrated here from the east some time between 8,000 and 3,000BC. Archaeological evidence suggests that, in the years leading up to the Danish invasion, the northern Estonian Rävala people lived a clan-like existence, engaged in fishing, farming and, increasingly, international trade. Present-day Tallinn was home to their port and marketplace, and by the 12th century they had built a wooden fortress on the steep limestone hill, Toompea, that rises over the area. In 1154 Arab cartographer Al-Idrisi marked the fortress on his map as a 'seasonal stronghold', the earliest mention of Tallinn in historic records.

That hilltop fortress saw plenty of action in the early 13th century, when the Pope's call for Christianisation of the Baltic Sea peoples touched off a bloody clash between Danes, Swedes, Germans and Russians, all scrambling to grab Baltic territory. In 1219, King Valdemar II of Denmark managed to capture the fortress on Toompea, marking the beginning of foreign domination in Estonia. From then on, every power that has ruled this land, from the Livonian Order to tsarist Russia to today's parliament, has done so from that same spot on the hill.

For the Danes, defeating the Estonians proved to be only half the battle. While Valdemar's troops were campaigning around Tallinn, the Order of the Brotherhood of the Sword, a group of German crusaders who had gained a foothold in Riga, fought their way northwards. They

Left: 15th-century Danish soldier in Tallinn
Right: detail, Town Hall door

pushed their way into the Danes' newly captured land, and tussles between the two powers ended with the Germans wresting away control of Toompea in 1227. A papal decree returned the fortress and Northern Estonia to the Danes in 1238, but not before the Knights of the Sword had founded a feudal system in the countryside, with German landlords as masters and the Estonians relegated to a near slave-like status as serfs. These new masters, the 'Baltic Germans', would remain the ruling class in Estonia for the next 700 years.

A German Town

During those early years, when the Order was carving up the Estonian countryside, it made another crucial move by inviting 200 German merchant families to settle at the base of Toompea Hill. The value of Tallinn's port was not lost on these industrious newcomers – they quickly turned their fledgling settlement into a commercial boomtown. They were so successful that in 1248 they were granted the right to adopt Lübeck law, effectively making the Lower Town a self-governing state. This arrangement led to a centuries-long split between Toompea Hill, home of the German landowners and representatives of whichever foreign power ruled Estonia (by now the Danes again), and the bustling merchant town below. Land squabbles and competing interests meant that citizens from the two areas were often at each other's throats, hence the high wall and gates between them. They remained administratively separate until 1887.

Glory Days

Tallinn's rapid growth in the 13th century produced the city sights such as St Nicholas', St Olav's, the Dome Church and the Dominican Monastery. The town's prospects brightened further, when, c.1284, it became a member of the Hanseatic League, a powerful alliance of trading cities that held a monopoly on commerce in Northern Europe. Because it occupied a pivotal spot on the shipping route to and from Russia, Tallinn was guaranteed a fortune trading in wax, grain, fur, linen, herring, wine and spices. The single most profitable commodity that came through the port was so-called 'white gold': salt.

Through its economic glory days of the 13th to 16th centuries, Tallinn continued to grow and flex the muscles of its autonomy. Members of the town council hardly batted an eyelid when, shortly after the doomed peasant rebellion known as the St George's Day Uprising, the Danes sold northern

Above: the Danes take Tallinn, 1219
Right: the capital as it looked in 1615

Estonia to the Riga-based Livonian Order in 1346; their independent status remained firmly intact under the new leadership.

However, Tallinn's increasing wealth was not shared among ethnic Estonians, who made up about half the population. This was very much a German-ruled town, officially known by its German name, *Reval*, until 1918. Even the Estonian name for the town, *Tallinn*, shows a lack of ownership – it's thought to be a contraction of *Taani Linn*, meaning 'Danish Castle'. Estonians were an economic underclass, confined to menial jobs. Yet life for town-dwelling Estonians was far better than the serfdom faced by their country cousins. The latter had one option for escape: Tallinn law declared that if an Estonian peasant managed to run off and hide in the town for a year and a day, evading capture by his master, he was considered free.

Caught Between Empires

Tallinn's fortune ran out in the mid-16th century at the onset of the Livonian War (1558–83). With the old Livonian state weakening, Russia, Poland, Denmark and Sweden moved in for a share of the Baltic pie. Though Tallinn surrendered to the Swedes in 1561, the war raged on for another 20 years. Tallinn's defensive walls and towers, built in the 14th century and improved since, proved their worth – Ivan the Terrible laid siege twice, but only managed to damage St Bridget's Convent and blow a hole in the top of Kiek in de Kök tower.

The 'Swedish Period' that followed turned out to be a mixed bag for the Tallinners. On the one hand, the Hanseatic town still had its independence and was engaged in trade, but, on the other, the war had taken its toll, and Tallinn had lost its lucrative position as the primary gateway to Russia. The city never managed to regain its pre-war economic prowess. For Estonians in the countryside though, things had never been better. The Swedes' relatively enlightened social policies increased the peasants' rights and established the country's first village schools. In 1632, King Gustav II Adolf founded Tartu University, which remains the nation's top educational institution. The Swedes were set to emancipate the serfs when history dealt the Estonians another blow, this time in the form of the Great Northern War.

Russian emperor Peter the Great's successful campaign to take the Baltic territories from Sweden lasted from 1700 to 1721, but for Tallinn, it ended

with surrender in 1710 and a devastating plague that killed over half the population of Estonia, reducing it to about 160,000. Even worse, incorporation into the Russian empire meant that Estonian peasants lost the rights they had gained under the Swedes, and were downgraded to the same property-like status as serfs in Russia. What Tallinn's high society saw, though, was a charismatic tsar who was infatuated with this seaside town. Peter made numerous visits, breaking ground on Kadriorg Palace and establishing the surrounding park – still Tallinners' favourite place to stroll – in 1718. Initially wooed by Peter, the local Baltic Germans retained their dominant social position over the next two centuries of tsarist rule, but their political power, especially in the city, was gradually waning.

Rise of the Estonians

Starting with the abolishment of serfdom in 1816, the lives of ethnic Estonians improved through the 19th century. The most crucial social development came from 1860 to 1880, when a widespread cultural revival known as the 'National Awakening' reached its height. Societies of 'Estophiles' began convincing Estonians that their language and culture, previously considered of little value, were things in which to take pride. Estonian choirs and theatrical societies were formed, the national epic, *Kalevipoeg*, was recorded and published, and the first Estonian-language newspaper, *Perno Postimees*, went into print. For the first time, Estonians began to think of themselves as a nation.

Spooked by increasing demands for self-rule in the Baltics, Tsar Aleksander III stepped up efforts to control and 'Russify' Estonia in the 1880s and '90s. It was at this time that the Aleksander Nevsky Cathedral, a powerful reminder of the empire's authority, was built.

But more profound changes were already taking place in Tallinn. The arrival of the rail line from St Petersburg in 1870 brought with it large-scale industry and an influx of thousands of Estonian and Russian workers. Huge factory complexes began to appear in the port area, and new tracts of wooden houses, like those in Kalamaja and Kopli, were built to accommodate the newcomers. As the population swelled, the town, now a city, started to take on a more Estonian character. In 1904, an Estonian-Russian political bloc beat out the Baltic Germans to win control of the city government. The city's premier house of culture, the Estonia Theatre, was completed in 1913. Around the nation, calls for Estonian autonomy were on the rise.

A New Republic

On 24 February 1918, with World War I raging and Russia embroiled in post-revolutionary chaos, Estonia declared itself independent. It would take a half-year of German occupation and a 13-month war against the Bolsheviks to ensure the new republic's survival.

Above: conscription of Estonians into the Russian army in the 19th century
Above right: 1930s' advertisement for pork products

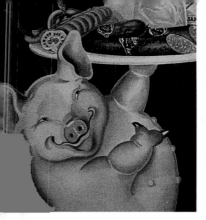

The years of the first Estonian republic were not easy. In the 1920s the economy was in poor shape, and political conflicts between ultra-left and ultra-right were threatening to tear society apart. In 1934, Estonia's head of state, Konstantin Päts, led a coup d'état to prevent a right-wing takeover. Despite his authoritarian rule, he remained popular and was made president in 1938. Business picked up in the post-depression 1930s, and the Estonian economy continued to improve, creating a standard of living that reached the European average. Impressive office buildings, such as those around Freedom Square, were first built. At the end of the decade, however, the clouds of war were again gathering over Europe.

War and Occupation

It's hard to overstate the impact that World War II and the subsequent Soviet occupation had on this tiny nation. The 22-year experiment with statehood ended abruptly in June 1940, when the Soviets invaded Estonia and absorbed it into the USSR. An horrific period of mass arrests and executions followed. On a single night in June 1941, 10,205 Estonians, mainly women and children, were rounded up, loaded into cattle cars and deported to Siberia. Under such circumstances, it's not surprising that the Nazis were initially greeted as liberators when they drove the Soviets out at the end of the year.

The Nazis fell out of favour, however, when it was clear that they had no plans to restore Estonia's independence. Soon the new regime's own harsh tactics came to light – during their three-year occupation they murdered 4,000 Jews, executed 7,000 Estonian citizens suspected of being Soviet collaborators and forced thousands into military service. Others joined the German ranks voluntarily, fearing another Soviet invasion.

On 9 March 1944, in an attempt to beat back the Germans, Soviet planes bombed Tallinn, killing over 900 people and leaving thousands homeless. St Nicholas' Church was flattened and the area around the Old Town's Harju Street was turned to rubble. When the Soviets finally managed to reinvade in September, 70,000 Estonians fled to the West to keep their culture alive in exile. At the same time, about 35,000 others escaped into Estonia's wilderness. Living rough, these 'Forest Brothers' formed an armed guerrilla movement that lasted until the mid-1950s.

Those that stayed had their worst fears realised in the form of Stalinist repression and forced collectivisation. A second mass deportation on 25 March 1949 exiled another 20,779 Estonians to Siberia. Meanwhile the Soviet regime began to resettle hundreds of thousands of ethnic Russians

Right: the bastion known as Fat Margaret on fire in 1917

in Estonia. Ostensibly they were needed to work in new factories that were built here, but they were also part of a policy of Russification, an attempt to sideline Estonians by making them the minority culture.

Relative calm returned in the 1950s after Stalin's death, and over the next four decades Tallinn's population grew. Large apartment block districts of Mustamäe, Õismäe and Lasnamäe sprang up to accommodate more incoming workers. Tallinn was spruced up when it played host to the sailing events of the 1980 Moscow Olympics; the TV tower, Linnahall harbour complex and Olümpia Hotel were all built for the occasion. Meanwhile, new generations either embraced the Soviet system or simply endured, celebrating Christmas in secret and occasionally tuning in to Finnish TV for a glimpse of life on the other side of the Iron Curtain.

From Independence to 'E-stonia'

During the *perestroika* years of 1987–88, what started as environmental protests quickly grew into mass demonstrations against Soviet control. In the summer of 1988, these culminated in a series of gigantic, semi-spontaneous singing events based on the tradition of Estonia's National Song Festivals. Crowds numbering from 100,000 to 300,000 – a fifth of the nation's population – packed Tallinn's Song Festival Grounds to express their national identity through folk songs and, increasingly, to call for independence from the USSR. The events of that summer came to be known as the 'Singing Rev-

olution'. Three years of defiance followed, with Estonia's communist officialdom supporting the movement and eventually proclaiming autonomy from Moscow. On 20 August 1991, during the failed coup against Gorbachev, Estonia declared independence from the crumbling Soviet Union.

The speed at which Estonia managed to dust off the Soviet grey and rebuild in the 1990s is one of the great success stories of modern Europe. An initial period of chaos and hyperinflation was brought under control thanks to bold economic reforms and foreign investment, not to mention an injection of Western know-how from returning 'foreign Estonians' (children of those who escaped in 1944). By the mid-1990s, economic growth in this 'Baltic Tiger' had blown past everyone's expectations. By 2004, Estonia had become a member of the EU. Curiously, much of its success was built on a foundation of internet and mobile technology, to which Estonians have taken like ducks to water. So wired is this little nation that international journalists have taken to calling it 'E-stonia'.

The effect of this breakneck economic transformation on Tallinn's skyline has also been profound, and, judging by the number of construction cranes in the area, even more gleaming new high-rises are on the way. Thankfully though, most corners of Tallinn remain untouched, and still resonate with that uncanny timelessness that makes the city so attractive.

Above: internet access in one of Europe's most hi-tech cities

HISTORY HIGHLIGHTS

3,000 BC Finno-Ugric tribes move to the Baltic area, mixing with existing Neolithic population.

1st century AD Roman Historian Tacitus writes of a people called Aestii.

11th century Estonians establish a wooden fortress on Toompea Hill.

1154 First mention of Tallinn in records by Arab cartographer, Al-Idrisi.

1219 Danish King Valdemar II captures the fortress on Toompea and goes on to conquer northern Estonia.

1227–38 Riga-based Germans temporarily take control from the Danes; Baltic Germans settle in Toompea; they rule the country for the next 700 years.

13th century A period of rapid growth; major landmarks are built, including St Nicholas' Church and the Dominican Monastery.

1248 Tallinn adopts Lübeck law, which makes it a self-governing trade city and effectively separates it from Toompea.

1284 Tallinn becomes a member of the Hanseatic League.

1343–5 Estonian peasants stage a St George's Night Uprising, a massive but unsuccessful rebellion against foreign rule.

1346 Danes sell their Estonian holdings to German knights in Riga, giving control to the Riga-based Livonian Order.

1404 Tallinn's current Town Hall is built.

1558–83 Livonian War between Russia, Poland, Sweden and Denmark leaves Estonia under Swedish rule.

1632 Tartu University founded, as part of enlightened Swedish educational policies.

1684 Fire devastates Toompea.

1710 Sweden loses Estonia to Russia in the Great Northern War (1700–21).

1718 Kadriorg Palace is completed.

1816 Serfdom abolished in Estonia.

1860–80 National Awakening sets stage for independence movement.

1870 St Petersburg–Tallinn railway completed; large-scale industrial growth follows.

1877 Toompea is administratively reunited with lower town.

1900 Aleksander Nevski Cathedral consecrated.

1918 Estonia declares independence from Russia, but only seals it after a 13-month war with Bolsheviks.

1940 Soviets invade Estonia and annex it into the USSR. Terror and mass deportations begin.

1941–43 Nazi invasion and occupation.

1944 A Soviet bombing raid kills 900 and destroys parts of the Old Town, including St Nicholas' Church. Soviet forces re-invade later that year; a half-century of Soviet occupation follows.

1949 A mass deportation on 25 March sends nearly 21,000 Estonians to Siberia.

1960s–80s The massive residential areas of Mustamäe, Õismäe and Lasnamäe are developed to accommodate incoming Russian workers.

1980 Tallinn hosts yachting events of the Moscow Olympics. The Olümpia Hotel, Olympic Yachting Centre, TV-Tower and Linnahall are built specially for the occasion.

1987–8 Mass protests against Soviet rule, later to be collectively called the 'Singing Revolution'.

1991 Estonia declares independence.

1994 Last Soviet troops leave Estonian territory.

2001 Estonia wins the Eurovision Song Contest and hosts the competition the following year, when Latvia wins.

2004 Estonia becomes a member of the European Union and joins NATO.

2008 Estonia pledged to adopt the euro.

Central Tallinn

300 m /330 yds

- ••••• Itinerary 1
- ••••• Itinerary 2
- ••••• Itinerary 3
- ••••• Itinerary 5
- ••••• Itinerary 10

Orientation

Tallinn is compact and easy to explore, with all the major sights clustered in and around its Old Town. This centuries-old maze of cobblestone streets, curious façades, Gothic churches and hidden courtyards – all protected by a medieval defensive wall and towers – is the city's biggest attraction. It's also a hive of social activity, home to the city's best restaurants and bars. The Old Town is divided into two distinct areas: the Lower Town, the former domain of a bustling Hanseatic trade city, and the more peaceful Toompea Hill, site of Toompea Castle and the grand houses of Estonia's Baltic German nobility. Brushing up against the Lower Town's southeast edge is Tallinn's small commercial centre, where shopping malls and most large hotels are located. Kadriorg Park lies just beyond, within reasonable walking distance.

The basic rules for touring Tallinn are: prepare for rain, even if the sky is clear, and don't start too early. This is a city of late risers, where most museums and attractions only open at 10 or 11am. Day-long itineraries in this guide are based on late-morning starts. When planning though, remember that it can be dangerous in park areas after sunset, and that Mondays and/or Tuesdays are closing days for most museums. Also, fashionistas should keep in mind that while local women may have inherited the ability to walk on the cobblestones of the Old Town in high heels, similar attempts by foreigners usually prove disastrous. Sturdy walking shoes are essential.

The Routes

The first three itineraries cover the Old Town's major sights and museums. Each is designed to last a full day, including time out for meals and shopping breaks, and is aimed at the curious visitor who likes to see everything. By skipping all the indoor attractions, however, it's perfectly feasible to combine the three itineraries and rush through the Old Town in a single day; this would leave more time to visit Tallinn's key park area, Kadriorg, addressed in the fourth tour. The remaining itineraries complete the Tallinn picture by exploring fascinating historical sites and intriguing outlying areas, some of which can only be reached by bus or taxi. Once on location, though, all itineraries are easily followed on foot.

Additionally, this guide includes four excursions that will take you beyond the city limits – to Helsinki, the bustling Finnish capital; Haapsalu, a relaxing, seaside resort town; Naissaar, an island littered with the eerie remnants of a Soviet military base; and the vast Lahemaa National Park, an antidote to urban tourism. A car is needed to explore Lahemaa, but the other destinations can be reached using regular ferry or coach connections.

Left view of St Olav's from Toompea Hill
Right: the Three Sisters, on Pikk Street

1. AROUND TOWN HALL SQUARE *(see map pages 18–19)*

On this day-long introduction to medieval Tallinn, you'll visit the most fascinating sights in and around the Old Town's main square, including the 15th-century Town Hall, two stunning churches and one of Europe's oldest pharmacies. You'll also hear some of the area's bizarre tales along the way.

Without a doubt, the best place to start exploring Tallinn is **Town Hall Square** (Raekoja plats), the spiritual and cultural heart of the city. This picture-postcard square, surrounded by medieval merchant houses, is where the cobblestone streets converge, where people from all walks of life mingle, and where concerts and craft fairs are held. In spring and summer, the square comes alive with crowded outdoor cafés and groups of tourists. It also plays host to Tallinn's Christmas Market each December, when it holds the town's Christmas tree, a tradition that dates back to 1441.

The Heart of the City

In medieval times, Town Hall Square served as both the centre of Tallinn's civic life and as its main marketplace (a two-storey weighhouse stood in the southwest corner until it was bombed in 1944). It was also the site of at least one execution. When the summer terraces aren't covering it, you can find **two stones** forming an 'L' in the area of the square near the Kehrwieder café. They mark the spot where, in the late 17th century,

Above: Town Hall Square
Left: dragon-headed gargoyle on the Town Hall

a drunken priest named Panicke was beheaded for killing a waitress with an axe. According to the story, he flew into a murderous rage after she served him an omelette that was 'as hard as the sole of a shoe'.

An equally noteworthy, and much less macabre, spot on the square is the so-called '**Centre of Tallinn**'. To find it, stand at right angles to the Town Hall's clock and the nearby Davidoff cigar house, then search the ground for a polished, round stone decorated with a compass rose. Text around its edges in Estonian and Latin proclaims that this is the 'zero point' of the Old Town. Whether this is the area's true geographical centre is debateable, but what makes this spot interesting is that from here you can see the tops of Tallinn's five most famous spires…with a bit of luck. Accomplishing the feat usually requires some gymnastics, but successfully facing the challenge has become something of a rite of passage for first-time visitors.

Key to the City

The grand, limestone building you see lording over the square is the **Town Hall** (Raekoda; open July–Aug Mon–Sat 10am–4pm; admission charge), workplace of Tallinn's all-powerful Town Council until 1889, and office of the city government until 1970. The late-Gothic structure was completed in 1404, though records show that previous town hall buildings stood on this spot as early as 1322. **Old Thomas** (Vana Toomas), the guard-shaped weather vane at the top of the spire, has been on duty since 1530, and has long been a symbol of the town. The fanciful, dragon-headed gargoyles were added in 1627. A peek at the interior is essential, but bear in mind that the Town Hall is only open in July and August; at other times of the year it's crucial that you book your visit ahead of time by phone (tel: 6457 900) or e-mail (raekoda@tallinnlv.ee).

You'll enter the building through the **Cellar Hall** (open mid-May–end June and Sept–mid-Oct Tues–Sat 11am–5pm; July–Aug Mon–Sat 10am–4pm; admission charge). This former wine cellar hosts history-related exhibitions and, unlike the rest of the Town Hall, is open throughout the tourist season.

The Town Hall's most impressive rooms are upstairs. The colourful, vaulted Citizens' Hall was used for festive occasions and is decorated with tapestries and Tallinn's coats of arms. Adjoining it, the **Council Hall** served both as a courtroom and a meeting room. Here, the powerful Town Council decided everything from issues of foreign policy to what fashions townsfolk could wear. Today the room houses the ceremonial key to the city and art treasures, including 17th-century paintings by Lübeck master Johann Aken and, more famously, a number of exquisitely decorated wooden benches dating from the 14th and 15th centuries. Intricate carvings on them depict stories such as Tristan and Isolde, Samson battling with a lion, and David and Goliath. Don't miss the comical scene of Phyllis riding on Aristotle's back.

Right: close up of the Town Hall

On the same floor you can also visit the Town Hall's *kämmerie*, a kind of accounting office, and its medieval kitchen (note the clever plumbing system). A new spiral staircase leads up through the kitchen's massive chimney, ending at the building's vast attic, where there are panel displays on the Town Hall's 20th-century history.

If you want to take a break after touring the Town Hall, you can get excellent coffee and pastries in the tiny, cave-like **Tristan and Isolde Café**, located on the left corner of the building as you face it from the square.

You may need the caffeine boost because next you have the option to climb the 64-m (210-ft) **Town Hall Tower** (Raekoja Torn; open mid-May–mid-Aug daily 11am–6pm; admission charge), which has a separate entrance at the base of the Town Hall. With its steep steps it's a tough climb (especially coming down), but the view from the top is unforgettable.

Photography and Pharmacy

The small alley directly behind the Town Hall is home to the **Town Prison–Museum of Photography** (Raevangla Fotomuuseum; open Mar–Oct Thur–Tues 10.30am–6pm; Nov–Feb Thur–Tues 10.30am–5pm; admission charge). The museum concentrates on Tallinn's 150-year-long love affair with photography, displaying a large collection of antique cameras and other photographic artefacts. You don't have to be a photo enthusiast to enjoy the museum – history buffs will appreciate its intriguing, pre-war images of the city and the fact that, in the 15th century, this was the town prison. The shape of the original cells can still be seen in the cellar exhibition room.

Directly across the square from here stands the **Town Hall Pharmacy** (Raeapteek; open Mon–Fri 9am–7pm, Sat 9am–5pm; admission free), one of the oldest continuously running pharmacies in Europe. The earliest mention of it in historical records dates it to 1422, though it's probably decades older. The institution has a fascinating history – ten generations of the same family, the Burcharts, operated it from 1581 to 1911. In medieval times, useful remedies available here included mummy juice, burnt bees and even

powdered unicorn horn (guaranteed to boost male potency). The shop also sold everyday items such as jam, gunpowder, tea, claret, confetti and marzipan. Today, the pharmacy retains its old-fashioned look but sells more familiar, modern curatives. In its small museum visitors can see 19th-century scales, bottles of archaic medicines and packaged drugs from the 1930s.

An archway next to the pharmacy leads to a lane whose name – **Saiakang** – means White Bread Passage, after the bakers' shops that operated here in medieval times. The tiny, red house at No. 4 is one of the smallest – and most photographed – buildings in the Old Town. It's now home to a sandwich shop that belongs to the Kehrweider Café just opposite, itself a worthy stop because of its cosy atmosphere. If you're looking for a more substantial meal break though, note that most restaurants around the square are, inevitably, tourist traps. To find some better options nearby, read further in this itinerary or visit any of the Old Town restaurants recommended under 'Eating Out'.

Spirits, Holy and Restless

Saiakang will bring you to a stunning white church with an octagonal tower. This is the **Holy Spirit Church** (Püha Vaimu Kirik; open to tourists May–Aug Mon–Sat 9am–5pm; Sept Mon–Sat 10am–4pm; Oct–Apr Mon–Fri 10am–3pm; admission charge), arguably the most important religious institution in medieval Tallinn. Founded in the 14th century as part of the adjacent Holy Spirit almshouse, which tended to the town's elderly, sick and poor, this was primarily a church of the common folk. It was here that the first sermons were read in Estonian after the Reformation, and in 1535 the church's pastor, Johann Koell, translated and published a catechism that's thought to be the first book in Estonian. Balthasar Russow, the chronicler from whom so much of Tallinn's history is known, served as pastor here from 1566 to 1600. The church also played a vital role in the city's administrative and commercial life; it served as the chapel for the Town Council, and one of its back rooms was used for signing contracts, the belief being that neither party would dare go back on a deal made in the presence of God.

The building itself, with its unique stepped gables, dates from the 1360s. Its Baroque spire, however, is a more recent addition – it replaced its Renaissance-style predecessor after a fire in 1684. The most striking external feature of the church is the blue-and-gold clock next to the main door. Created in the late 17th century by master woodcarver Christian Ackermann, it's Tallinn's oldest, and by far most famous, public timepiece. The figures in each of its corners represent the four apostles.

Left: picturesque Saiakang (White Bread Passage)
Above: pharmacy sign. **Right:** clock, Holy Spirit Church

Even more impressive is the church's carved-wood interior. Here you'll find elaborate galleries covered with painted panels, a fine Renaissance pulpit from 1597 and the church's pride and joy: the folding altar created by Lübeck master Bernt Notke in 1483.

If you're in the mood for a shopping break after leaving the church, head across the street to **Börsi Käik**, an alley in which a crafts market operates in summer. Also note that as you head left up Pikk Street, you'll pass the highest concentration of souvenir shops in Tallinn.

Once on **Ratasekaevu** (Wheel Well Street), you'll find some decent lunch options. **Kompressor**, the casual bar at No. 3, is a favourite among students for its enormous, filled pancakes. For something more old-fashioned and involved, try the grandma-themed **Vanaema Juures** at Rataskaevu 10, or the village-style **Kuldse Notsu Kõrts**, just around the corner on Dunkri.

After a few steps down Rataskaevu, you'll reach the picturesque, covered **wheel well** that gives the street its name. It has a strange legend attached to it: in medieval times, superstitious Tallinners believed that a spirit that lived in the well would flood the town unless it was fed regular animal sacrifices. Because most victims were the Old Town's stray cats – which were flung, usually live, down the well – locals began calling this the Cat's Well. The town never flooded, but nor did the water quality improve, and eventually the well was filled in.

Look directly across the street at Rataskaevu 16 to see an oddly bricked-up window on the top floor. This is the so-called 'Devil's Wedding' house, the source of Tallinn's most famous ghost story. For decades, strange party noises were said to be heard emanating from this apartment late at night. According to a well-known Tallinn tale, a mysterious man, who later turned out to be the Devil, once rented the room for his wedding party.

St Nicholas' Church

Rataskaevu ends at the towering **St Nicholas' Church** (Niguliste Kirik), whose square tower absolutely dwarfs the buildings that surround it. Dedicated to the patron saint of merchants and artisans, it was founded c.1230 by German settlers who operated a trade yard in the area. Because it predates the town's defensive wall, it was built with heavy wooden beams to bar its doors and hiding places for use during an attack. Interestingly, this was the only church in Lower Town that escaped ransacking by Reformationist mobs in 1524, mainly thanks to the quick thinking of the head of its congregation, who poured molten lead into the locks.

Though the building's main body and choir date to a major 15th-century expansion, the appearance of St Nicholas' today is mainly the result of constant rebuilding in later years. In fact, the church was destroyed by Soviet bombs in World War II, then meticulously reconstructed from 1956 to 1984.

It now serves as the **Niguliste Museum–Concert Hall** (open Wed–Sun 10am–5pm; admission charge), which displays church art from around Estonia. In addition to medieval tombstones, altarpieces and sculptures, its collection includes Tallinn's most famous painting, a fragment of Bernt Notke's late 15th-century masterpiece *Dance Macabre (Dance with Death)*. The eerie mural, which shows people from all walks of life, rich and poor, dancing with skeletons, is a reminder that in death we are all equal.

While here, don't miss the **Silver Chamber**, where beautiful items from Tallinn's guilds are on display, and the photo exhibit on the church's history near the entrance. You can also return to hear one of the 30-minute organ concerts held here every Saturday and Sunday at 4pm. In summer, additional concerts take place at 1pm.

Soviet Bombsite

Heading right as you exit the church will bring you down the steps to Harju, a street hard hit during the infamous Soviet bombing raid of 9 March 1944. That attack, which killed over 900 people and left 20,000 homeless, was covered over, literally and figuratively, during the Soviet era – damage was simply blamed on 'fascist aggression', and the large, empty area on the right side of the street was turfed over. It was only later, in the heady days of the late 1980s independence movement that the spot was uncovered, and now you can see cellars and foundations of the buildings that were destroyed.

The tour ends here at the corner of Harju and Müüri-vahe, but there are a number of opportunities for you to continue. If you're interested in seeing more museums, you can visit the odd and somewhat musty **Theatre and Music Museum** (Müürivahe 12; open Wed–Sun 10am–6pm; admission charge), home of antique instruments and music boxes. Beyond it is a large junction that takes you to Suur-Karja and more Old Town meandering. If you're hungry, you can instead turn right to reach the Grillhaus Daube restaurant at Rüütli 11, or turn left onto Müüri-vahe, where you can relax in Lounge 8 or Reval Café.

Above left: pulpit inside the Holy Spirit Church. **Left:** Old Town backstreet
Right: St Nicholas' Church

2. PIKK AND THE LATIN QUARTER *(see map pages 18–19)*

Exploration of the Lower Town continues with a journey down Pikk, a street that is home to medieval guild halls, weird and wonderful façades, the lofty St Olav's Church and Fat Margaret's Tower. The tour then takes you through the Latin Quarter and the ruins of the 13th-century Dominican Monastery and the attractive St Catherine's Passage.

In medieval times, **Pikk jalg**, or 'Long Street', was a bustling, commercial thoroughfare linking the town's port to its main marketplace on Town Hall Square. True to its name, it was the longest street in Tallinn, and, more significantly, home to Tallinn's all-important merchant and craft guilds. These powerful associations not only regulated professional activity in Tallinn, they also played a key part in the town's administrative and social life.

Great Guild

The most prominent and elite of these guilds was the Great Guild, whose headquarters was the **Great Guild Hall** (Suurgildi hoone) at Pikk 17. Made up of the town's wealthiest (married) German merchants, the Great Guild was a rich, politically influential organisation – the mayor and all members of the Town Council were chosen from its ranks. The size and grandeur of its meeting hall leaves no doubt as to the guild's relative status. Built c.1410, this was the largest secular building in medieval Tallinn apart from the Town Hall itself. The red-and-white emblems you see on its façade are the guild's coat of arms; the lion's-head knockers on its doors date to 1430.

Take a look at the hall's spacious, vaulted interior by visiting the **Estonian History Museum** (open Thur–Tues 11am–6pm; admission charge), which

Top: entrance to Pikk Street
Above: door knocker on the Great Guild

is now housed here. Though not extensive, the museum covers the nation's history from Neolithic times up to the 18th century. Don't miss the two lunette paintings, dating to 1869, in the side room.

Famous Café

Directly across from the Great Guild stands Tallinn's oldest and most famous café, **Maiasmokk** (Sweet Tooth), which has been causing cavities since 1864. Drop in for a peek at its beautiful, old-fashioned ceiling. At the right end of this building you'll find the small **Kalev Marzipan Museum Room** (open Mon–Sat 10am–7pm, Sun 10am–5pm; admission charge), where you can see confectioners working on intricate marzipan creations.

One of Tallinn's wildest façades, complete with seahorse-like dragons and bare-breasted Egyptian slaves, can be found on the **Dragon Gallery** next door, at Pikk 18. Tartu-born artist Jacques Rosenbaum created it in 1910, when this kind of Art Nouveau flamboyance was in vogue.

The triple-gabled **Kanut Guild Hall** (Kanuti Gildi hoone) at Pikk 20 presents a very different architectural style. This was home to the Kanut Guild, whose members were skilled craftsmen from a number of different trades. Though the building is much older, its English-inspired Tudor façade comes from a remodelling in 1863–64, at which time the statues of St Kanut and Martin Luther were added. The hall has recently found new life as a modern dance theatre.

At this point, if you stand at the front of the guild hall and look up across the street, you'll spot the stern face of a man staring back at you through lorgnette glasses. This is the so-called **peeping man**, at Pikk 25. The figure's origin is the subject of many theories, the most interesting of which claims that a jealous wife installed it to break her husband's habit of spying on the ladies practising ballet on the upper floors of the guild hall.

Brotherhood of Blackheads

At Pikk 26 you'll come to the ornamental, Dutch Renaissance-style **House of the Brotherhood of Blackheads** (Mustpeademaja; open daily 10am–7pm; admission charge). The Brotherhood, whose members were unmarried German merchants, was a vital institution in medieval Tallinn, responsible for the town's defence as well as for organising festivals and tournaments. Its name comes from the fact that its patron, St Mauritius, was a Moor. His profile, the symbol of the Brotherhood, can be seen on the building's green-, red-and-gold main door, which dates to 1640. The rest of the façade was erected in 1597. The building is used for meetings and concerts, but on event-free days you can explore its vaulted halls and courtyard.

A cluster of restaurants along this stretch provides a great opportunity for lunch. The Golden Dragon at Pikk 37 is considered to be the city's

Right: young Estonian

best Chinese restaurant, while the Hell Hunt pub next to it serves great inexpensive meals.

While having lunch, you may want to steel your nerves with a drink, because down the street at No. 59 is a spot that sends shivers down the spines of many who pass. The building, with its bricked-up basement windows, originally housed Estonia's War Department, but after the Soviet takeover in 1940 it became Tallinn's **KGB headquarters**. It was here that perceived enemies of the regime were taken and processed before being shot or sent to Siberian work camps. Now the only clue to its dark past is a plaque that reads, 'This building housed the headquarters of the organ of repression of the Soviet occupational power. Here began the road to suffering for thousands of Estonians.'

St Olav's

A few steps further is the gigantic **St Olav's Church** (Oleviste Kirik), which is more easily seen with a quick detour down Oleviste Street. First mentioned in records in 1267, it's thought to have served a group of Scandinavian merchants who camped on this end of Pikk Street in the 12th century. The church's overall shape comes from a 15th-century rebuilding, but c.1500, an absurdly tall 159-m (522-ft) Gothic-style pavilion steeple was added, which made this the tallest building in the world from 1549 to 1625.

The lofty spire was presumably meant to act as a signpost for ships approaching the busy trade town. Whether or not it was effective in that regard, it made an excellent lightning rod, attracting numerous lightning strikes over the years and causing the church to burn to the ground three times. The current steeple was installed after the first of these fires in 1625, and is only 124m (407ft) tall, 25m (82ft) shorter than the original. To get a better idea of the church's height, you can make the gruelling climb up its tower (open Apr–Oct daily 10am–6pm; admission charge). Once you catch your breath you'll be rewarded with views of Toompea and the Old Town.

A far smaller but equally impressive sight can be found nearby at Pikk 71, site of the much-loved **Three Sisters** (Kolm õde), a wonderfully restored trio of 15th-century residence houses. Though notoriously hard to photograph on this narrow street, the ensemble's façade, including the elaborate, baroque door dating to 1651, represents the town's medieval architecture at its most beautiful. The buildings now accommodate a chic hotel *(see pages 88–89)*.

Fat Margaret

Pikk Street ends at the **Great Coast Gate** (Suur Rannaväravad). Along with the Viru Gates, this is all that remains of the six powerful entrances that once controlled access to medieval Tallinn. The Great Coast Gate, in fact

Above: St Olav's
Right: the Three Sisters

a system of gates and towers, originated in the early 1300s, but its largest component, **Fat Margaret** (Paks Margareeta; *see page 47*), was built from 1511 to 1530. The source of the tower's unusual name is unclear – some claim it has to do with the squat shape of the building; others insist that Margaret was a cook who once worked here. In any case, with its 25-m (82-ft) diameter and walls up to 5m (16ft) thick, the four-storey cannon tower provided the town with formidable protection from attacks on its seaward side.

Fat Margaret's imposing shape is really only visible from the other side of the gate, but before leaving Pikk Street, you can drop into the **Estonian Maritime Museum** (open Wed–Sun 10am–6pm; admission charge), housed inside Fat Margaret. Apart from giving you an idea of just how impressively sturdy the tower looks from the inside, the museum presents extensive displays detailing Estonia's seafaring history from Neolithic times to the present. While here, you may want to head up to the roof for a beautiful view of the Old Town and the port area, particularly if you opted out of climbing the much more challenging St Olav's Church tower earlier on in this tour.

After passing through the Great Coast Gate, follow the curve of the tower around to the right and into a small park area. Here you'll see some antique cannons perched at the edge of the hill, and a large monument in the shape of an incomplete bridge. The latter is a memorial to the victims of the *Estonia* ferry disaster. On 28 September 1994, 852 people died when the 15,000-tonne passenger ship sank en route from Tallinn to Stockholm.

From here a set of wooden stairs leads downhill to the right. At its bottom is a rather unusual branch of the Maritime Museum, the **Mine Museum** (open Wed–Sun 9am–5pm; admission charge). It hosts a somewhat disturbing collection of sea mines (all safely deactivated), some dating back to the late 1800s. These deadly leftovers from various wars still litter the Baltic Sea and continue to wash up on Estonia's beaches.

In case you haven't yet eaten by this point, or just want a break, note that the casual, vibrantly decorated African Kitchen at Uus 34 serves excellent and surprisingly cheap meals. Shortly after passing it, you'll have to veer right, then turn left to reach Vene Street, where our route continues.

city itineraries

Where Monks Roamed

The area you're now entering is known as the Latin Quarter, so named because the town's legendary Dominican Monastery is its central feature. The street's name, Vene (meaning 'Russian'), however, comes from the presence of the Russian **St Nicholas Orthodox Church** (open daily 9.30am–5pm), on your left at No. 24. The church was first founded on this site in 1442 in connection with a Russian market that operated here, but the magnificent building you see now, with its dome and twin belltowers, was designed by St Petersburg architect Luigi Rusca and built 1820–27. Drop in to get a glimpse of its famed iconostas, one of the most impressive in Estonia.

A few steps further brings you to the **Tallinn City Museum** (Tallinna Linnamuuseum; open Mar–Oct Wed–Mon 10.30am–6pm; Nov–Feb Wed–Mon 10.30am–5pm; admission charge), in a grand, medieval merchant house at Vene 17. This modern and innovative museum provides an excellent way to get acquainted with the various periods of the town's development. Don't miss the collection of World War II propaganda posters on its top level.

When you head into the courtyard at Vene 18 you'll face the pseudo-Gothic Sts Peter and Paul Roman Catholic Church, completed in 1844, but your real destination is Vene's main attraction: the **Dominican Monastery** (Dominiklaste Klooster; open mid-May–late Sept daily 9.30am–6pm; admission charge), with an entrance on the right-hand side of the yard. Known as St Catherine's Monastery, it was founded by the Dominican Order in 1246, and played a central role in medieval Tallinn's ecclesiastical life for nearly three centuries. The monastery was closed during the Reformation in 1525, and in 1531, the abandoned compound was gutted by fire.

Today what remains are its beautiful stone courtyard, three surrounding ambulatories and some interior chambers. The Dominican Monastery Museum encompasses the building's outdoor section, and displays a collection of Tallinn's medieval stonemasonry. Save the metal amulet you're given upon entry – it entitles you to free admission to the museum for life. You'll get a chance to see the monastery's inner rooms later on this tour.

St Catherine's Passage

Pass through the small archway at Vene 12 to reach one of the most picturesque spots in Tallinn, **St Catherine's Passage** (Katariina käik), a narrow lane wedged between the remains of St Catherine's Church and a jumble of 15th- to 17th-century residential buildings. What makes the lane even more interesting is that it's home to **St Catherine's Guild** (Katariina Gild), an association of artisans who operate a row of open studio/ workshops along the passage's left side. Visitors are welcome to drop into any of their shops to browse

Above: quiet spot, Dominican Monastery
Right: working at St Catherine's Guild

round their creations, pick up a gift or two or watch the artists at work on silk screening, ceramics, leather-making, quilting, blown-glass and other crafts.

On the passage's left-hand side, a curious collection of stone burial slabs, rescued from St Catherine's Church, is on display. The first one, on the left as you face them, is unique in that it's Tallinn's oldest-known burial slab for a woman. You can make out her portrait if you look closely.

Dominican Monastery Claustrum

The passage ends at Müürivahe, where a left turn will take you to the **Dominican Monastery Claustrum** (Dominiklaste Kloostri Klausuur; Müürivahe 33; open mid-May–mid-Sept daily 10am–5pm; admission charge). A separate entity from the Monastery Museum, it allows visitors access to the monastery's fascinating inner rooms, including the monks' dormitory, library and refectory. Be sure to visit the cellar room, where a mysterious 'Energy Pillar' is said to bring physical and spiritual health.

A turn in the opposite direction down Müürivahe puts you at the Sweater Market, a section of the town wall where old ladies sell every kind of knitted creation imaginable. Here you can spend some time shopping, or head out to Viru Street, the Old Town's busiest pedestrian thoroughfare.

Our route ends at the Viru Gates, to your left as you reach Viru Street. The two round towers were once part of larger 14th-century gate system that stood at the end of the street, controlling entry on the town's eastern flank. Most of that gate was pulled down in 1888 to make way for traffic, but these two small towers remain and make a fitting entry into the Old Town.

Above: walking along the picturesque St Catherine's Passage

3. TOOMPEA *(see map pages 18–19)*

This route guides you through the upper portion of the Old Town, showing you Toompea Castle, Aleksander Nevsky Cathedral, the Dome Church and some spectacular views of the city.

Estonian mythology claims that Toompea, the limestone hill that rises above central Tallinn, is in fact the burial mound of the city's legendary founder, Kalev. After his death, so the story goes, his wife Linda was so grief-stricken that she kept piling more and more stones on his grave until, eventually, this entire 24-m (78-ft) hill was formed. Kalev or no Kalev, this is certainly an appropriate spot for a legend concerning the city's origins – Toompea is widely considered to be the historic birthplace of Tallinn. It was here that the ancient Estonians built their wooden fortress in the days before the first foreign invaders, sowing the seeds of the town's first permanent settlement.

An equally important facet of Toompea is that, for over 800 years, it has been the nation's seat of power. From the Danish conquerors in 1219, every state or empire that has ruled Estonia has done so using Toompea Castle as its base. The castle's occupants (Danes, Teutonic Knights, Swedes and Russians) shared Toompea with another ruling group, Estonia's Baltic German nobles, who maintained their lavish houses within the fortified space of the hill.

As the home of these powerful groups, Toompea remained separated from, and often at odds with, the independent trade town below. Even today it has a quieter, less commercial feel than the rest of the Old Town. It also retains its reputation as a place of power and wealth; it's home to Estonia's government, several embassies, and Tallinn's most expensive real estate.

Above: Aleksander Nevsky Cathedral

Short Leg Street

Our tour begins at the base of picturesque **Lühike jalg** (Short Leg Street), a narrow, cobbled lane, partly flanked by a staircase, that winds its way up the hill. In medieval times, it provided the main pedestrian access to Toompea. Now, apart from being a popular route for tourists, Lühike is a favourite destination for art lovers, thanks to the high concentration of galleries and shops here. It's also the site of the **Adamson-Eric Museum** (open Wed–Sun 11am–6pm; admission charge) at Lühike 3, near the bottom of the hill. Adamson-Eric (1902–68) was arguably the most dynamic and versatile artist in Estonian history. In the museum you'll see the bright, colourful works he created in a wide range of media, from oil painting to furniture design. After visiting the museum, you can peruse the art and design galleries on your way up the hill. As you do, be sure to visit the back room of the Lühikese Jala Galerii, which somewhat bizarrely has a natural spring stuck in one of its walls.

At the top of the street's 16-m (52-ft) climb you'll see the **Short Leg Gate Tower** (Lühikese jala vüravatorn), built in 1456. The tower underwent extensive renovation in the 1980s and now acts as a concert venue for Tallinn's acclaimed early music group, Hortus Musicus. When you pass through the gate, note its heavy, wooden door, an original from the 17th century.

Once you're through the gate, turn left and start uphill. The cosy Bogapott pottery shop and café on your left is a very decent place to stop for coffee or a snack, and is one of the few casual eating options on Toompea. The Pika Jala restaurant opposite Bogapott is pricier but also passable.

Aleksander Nevsky Cathedral

As you approach the top of the hill, a magnificent onion-domed church will come into view. This dreamy masterpiece is the **Aleksander Nevsky Cathedral** (open daily 8am–7pm; admission free), the most impressive Orthodox church in Estonia. It was built from 1894 to 1900 by renowned St Petersburg architect Mikhail Preobrazhensky, who based its design on the five-domed churches erected in Moscow and Yaroslavl from the 17th century.

Though the church now serves a purely religious purpose, it was originally placed here as a blatant symbol of Russian power. In the late 19th century, imperial Russia was carrying out an intense campaign of Russification in its Baltic territories, an attempt to exert cultural domination over the mainly Lutheran Estonians and Germans. As part of that drive, this massive Orthodox cathedral was constructed in this place of prominence, directly opposite Toompea Castle, on a spot that would make it visible from much of the town below. Very fittingly, the church was named after Aleksander Nevsky, the heroic Grand Duke of Novgorod who famously beat back the advancing Baltic Germans in the legendary 'Battle on the Ice' on Lake

Right: stained glass in the cathedral

Peipsi on the Estonian/Russian border in 1242. You can see a beautiful mosaic of him on the south face of the building.

In a typically surreal Tallinnesque twist, while the cathedral was still under construction, a rumour floated among superstitious locals that workmen digging its foundations had stumbled upon the tomb of old Kalev, which bore a warning that any further disturbance would prompt him to destroy the city. Even more weight was given to the tale when ominous cracks began to appear in the cathedral's base. As you can see, however, the expected disaster never came to pass.

Climb the church's steps to take a look at its awe-inspiring interior. While the faithful are lighting prayer candles, you can quietly make your way in to study the artworks, including the enormous gilded wooden iconostas and the 2-m (6½-ft) paintings of the apostles on the main cupola's arches. Be sure to note the elaborate chandeliers – they're based on those in the Moscow Kremlin.

Toompea Castle

Opposite the cathedral you'll see a regal pink building with an Estonian flag proudly flying above it. This is the **Toompea Castle** (Toompea Loss), the historic abode of Estonia's rulers and now, appropriately, home to Estonia's parliament. The castle traces its origins back to 1227–29, when the Knights of the Sword built a square stone fortress here to replace the earlier wooden strongholds of the Danes and the Estonians. In the 14th century, the castle was rebuilt as a convent-style structure with a trapezoidal courtyard, 20-m (65-ft) walls, and towers at each of its four corners. Three of those towers are still standing today.

You've probably noticed that the section of the building you're facing doesn't particularly look like a medieval castle. That's because this wing is in fact a baroque palace built from 1767 to 1773 on the orders of Catherine the Great. It served as the headquarters for Estonia's provincial administration in tsarist times. To get a better idea of the castle's medieval shape, you can take a break from this route and walk halfway down nearby Falgi tee for a different perspective. Barring that, find the sign on your left displaying an aerial photograph of the complex. The image will also show you the three-storey, expressionist-style parliament building, which was added to the inner courtyard in the early 1920s.

Above: interior and dome detail, Aleksander Nevsky Cathedral
Right: Toompea Castle walls and the Dome Church

Because of the castle's official function, visitors aren't allowed inside, but you can see more of the structure by visiting the tranquil **Governor's Garden** (Kuberneri Aed), accessible through the gates at the castle's left. From here you'll get the best view of another landmark, the castle's **Tall Hermann** (Pikk Hermann; *see also page 58*). The tower was built here at the southwest corner of the castle in 1371, but reached its current height of 48m (157ft) after reconstruction in 1500. It's a generally accepted principle that whichever nation flies its flag on Tall Hermann can claim to be the ruler of Estonia, so when the Estonian tricolour appeared here on 24 February 1989 instead of the Soviet banner, the act was regarded as a major triumph for the independence movement. The black-, blue-and-white flag has been flying here ever since, making this tower an important symbol of Estonia's statehood.

At this point, you may want to break for lunch. The nearest choices are the French-Russian-style Cathedral at Toom-Kooli 1, and the Toomkooli Restaurant at Toom-Kooli 13, at the end of a spur leading off to the street's left. Both are somewhat upmarket. For something less formal, the Greek-style Syrtaki Taverna nearby at Piisikopi 1 is an option.

Dome Church

Heading down Toom-Kooli Street brings you to Kiriku plats (Church Square), at the centre of which stands Estonia's main Lutheran church, the majestic, white **Dome Church** (Toomkirik; open daily 9am–5pm; admission free). Officially known as the Cathedral of St Mary the Virgin, this was historically the church of the Toompea elite. It's thought to have been founded as a wooden church after the Danish invasion of 1219, then rebuilt as a stone structure in the 1240s. What you see now is the result of several centuries of development. The church's vaulted main body, for example, originates from the 14th century, but the baroque tower is a later addition, dating to 1778–79.

As you enter the church, you'll notice that you have to take several steps downwards. This is a result of the devastating fire that ripped through Toompea in 1684. When the area was being rebuilt, it turned out that rubble from the fire had raised the street level by about a metre relative to the church's floor.

Once inside the main hall, you'll see that the walls are covered with funereal coats of arms, which date from the 17th to 20th centuries. Inscribed with epitaphs, they were used in the funeral processions of wealthy Baltic German families, then placed in the church as memorials. The church's elaborate baroque pulpit and high altar both date to 1696 and were carved by the renowned Tallinn sculptor, Christian Ackermann. Around the hall you'll also see the ornate tombs of several important historic figures. Among these is Pontus de la Gardie (d.1585), the French-born head of the Swedish forces during the Livonian War, whose last resting place is behind the altar. Along the wall opposite the doors are the tombs of A.J. von Krusenstern (d.1848), a Baltic German explorer who was the first to circumnavigate the globe under the Russian flag, and Admiral Samuel Greig of Fife, Scotland (1735–88), commander of Russia's Baltic fleet and supposed lover of Catherine the Great.

As you stepped into the church, you probably walked over the large burial slab of a less historic but more curious personage, Otto Johann Thuve. Sometimes referred to nowadays as 'Tallinn's Don Juan', Thuve was a notorious drinker and womaniser. Just before he died in 1696, he requested that he be buried here at the entrance to the church, so that those entering would have to tread over him, and in doing so help wash to away his sins.

Leaving the church and heading towards Kohtu Street, look left to see the green, Renaissance-style **Knighthood House**. It was built in 1848 to serve as a meeting place for the Knighthood, a kind of class authority for Toompea's gentry. Along Kohtu itself, you'll pass several extravagant neoclassical mansions built for these nobles, a testament to their fabulous wealth.

A View over the Rooftops

The street brings you to the **Kohtuotsa Viewing Platform**, which provides a stunning panorama of medieval Tallinn and the modern city centre beyond. From here you can spot the octagonal towers of the Town Hall and Holy Spirit Church below. On your extreme right you see the square tower of St Nicholas' Church, and on your left is the pointed spire of St Olav's. Off in the distance, along the shoreline, you can make out the curved roof of the Tallinn Song Festival Arena, and further along the coast, the triangular ruins of the Pirita Convent *(see page 48)*.

To reach the next viewing platform, walk a few paces straight back from here and turn right onto Toom-Rüütli. At its end, a narrow passage leads off to the left and brings you to the **Patkuli Viewing Platform**. Here you'll get another excellent view of the Lower Town, as well as a

picturesque stretch of Tallinn's medieval wall and towers, which you can visit in Itinerary 5 *(see page 44)*. If you want to see them close up at this point, or finish your Toompea tour here, you can head down the winding **Patkuli Steps** to Nunne Street.

To the left of the platform, the balcony of the neighbouring **Sten-**

Left: Government buildings on Toompea

bock House (Stenbocki Maja) is visible. This 18th-century manor has been, at various times, a courthouse and private residence but now serves as the office of the Government of Estonia. As you leave the viewing platform and proceed down Rahukohtu, you'll pass its front and a courtyard. On the building's outer wall hangs a memorial tablet to officials killed after the first Soviet invasion of 1940, victims of the systematic elimination of the republic's leadership.

Back to the Old Town

Cutting across Toompea via Rahukohtu and Piisikopi streets brings you back to the Aleksander Nevsky Cathedral. From here, **Pikk jalg** (Long Leg Street) leads downhill into Lower Town. Whereas Lühike jalg (Short Leg Street) provided access to Toompea for pedestrians, the long, straight Pikk was primarily used for carriage traffic. The four-sided tower at its bottom is the **Long Leg Gate Tower** (Pika jala väravatorn), built in 1380 and expanded in the mid-15th century. A study of this street will give you some idea of the level of mistrust between Toompea's residents and those in the Lower Town – the small windows on the tower's face are shooting vents, and the high wall to your right was called the 'Wall of Hatred'. These days, though, Pikk is simply known as one of the Old Town's most picturesque streets.

Above: Long Leg Gate Tower
Right: time out for a chat

4. KADRIORG (see map page 42)

On this stroll around the gardens and ponds of the leafy Kadriorg district, you'll explore the spectacular Kadriorg Palace, see the residence of the Estonian president and visit the city's major art museums.

From the Hobujaama stop in the centre, take tram 1 or 3 to the Kadriorg stop. Alternatively, you can walk here from the Old Town in about 20–25 minutes.

With its palaces, villas, parks and pathways, the quiet Kadriorg district, just outside the city centre, is easily Tallinn's favourite urban getaway – an ideal place to walk dogs, rollerskate, meet up with friends and exchange gossip. It also enjoys a reputation as one of the city's most prestigious neighbourhoods, an area with a long-standing connection to the upper crust of Tallinn society.

Kadriorg in fact owes its existence to one of Tallinn's most aristocratic visitors, Peter the Great. Just after conquering Estonia in the Great Northern War, the Russian emperor bought this land for use as a summer estate, which he named in honour of his wife, Catherine I. The area's name in Estonian (Kadri + *org*) actually means 'Catherine's Valley'.

Grand Designs

From the time of the estate's founding in 1718, its grounds have been open as a public park, and city dwellers have been free to stroll through its forests and gardens. Later years saw Kadriorg become more residential. Wealthy Tallinners began building grand villas here in the 19th century, and stylish, functionalist homes cropped up in the 1920s and '30s. Even today Kadriorg is an enviable address, one shared by the likes of TV celebrities and even Estonia's president. It's no surprise then that sightseers often come here just to marvel at the neighbourhood's elegant and varied architecture.

Above: Kadriorg Palace. **Left:** Catherine the Great
Right: taking a walk in Kadriorg Park

Recently, however, there has been another reason to visit – Kadriorg home to the largest branches of the Art Museum of Estonia.

Once you arrive at the Kadriorg tram stop, head straight across nearby Poska to find a picturesque, rectangular pond with an old-fashioned gazebo at its centre. This is the **Swan Pond**, a fittingly romantic introduction to the neighbourhood. Here you'll see flocks of ducks, swans and pigeons, usually concentrated around any visitor generous enough to throw them a few breadcrumbs. As you make your way around the pond's perimeter, you'll pass colourful flowerbeds, as well as a monument to Friedrich Reinhold Kreutzwald (1803–82), the physician and writer who published Estonia's national epic, the *Kalevipoeg*.

Catherine's Palace

Further along the street, on its opposite side, stands what is unquestionably the jewel in the crown of the park: the magnificent baroque **Kadriorg Palace** (Kadrioru Loss; open May–Sept Tues–Sun 10am–5pm; Oct–Apr Wed–Sun 10am–5pm; admission charge), built in 1718 on the order of Peter the Great. The palace was designed by Italian architect Niccolo Michetti and created in the style of an Italian villa, with a main building flanked by two annexes. The tsar named it Ekaterinenthal, or Catherinenthal, in honour of his wife, and intended it for use as a royal summer residence. In the end, his family hardly spent any time here at all.

Because the palace itself easily qualifies as an artistic masterpiece, it's very fitting that it's now home to the **Kadriorg Art Museum** (open Wed–Sun 10am–5pm; admission charge), which displays the Art Museum of Estonia's main collection of foreign works. Hundreds of treasured paintings by 16th- to 20th-century Western European and Russian artists are on display here, as are prints, sculptures and other decorative objects. When you enter the museum, consider purchasing a combined ticket that also covers the Mikkel Museum, which is next on this tour.

As you make your way around the palace to look at the artworks, you'll also gain insight into the world of tsarist extravagance. Particularly decadent is the two-storey main hall, with its flamboyant ceiling painting and rich stuccowork. It's considered to be one of the best examples of baroque design

in Northern Europe, and is likely to make your jaw drop. Also worth mentioning are the impressive rooms on the upper floor designed by architect Olev Siinmaa. They were used in the 1930s, when the palace served as the residence of Estonia's Head of State. After your tour of the building's interior, be sure to visit the beautiful, 18th-century-style flower garden, complete with shooting fountains, around the back.

If at this or any other point of the tour you feel the need for some nourishment, you can easily make your way back down Weizenbergi to the tram stop. Here you'll find the Cantina Carramba Tex-Mex restaurant and the Kadriorg Restaurant–Spaghetteria, both of which serve respectable fare. Note that Kadriorg Palace and the KUMU (covered opposite) also have cafés.

Mikkel Museum and the Presidential Palace

Just across the street from the palace, in its former kitchen house, is another branch of the Art Museum of Estonia, the **Mikkel Museum** (open Wed–Sun 11am–6pm; admission charge). Donated by private collector Johannes Mikkel in 1994, the museum's incredible collection includes more than 600 items,

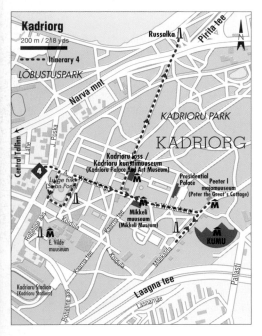

among them Flemish and Dutch paintings, Italian engravings and exquisite Chinese porcelain. The most prized works are four etchings by Rembrandt, one of which is a self-portrait.

Further up the street on the left is a building that at first glance looks like a smaller, plainer copy of the baroque palace you've just visited. This is in fact the **Presidential Palace**, the official residence and workplace of Estonia's president. Designed by the architect Alar Kotli and completed in the summer of 1938, it accommodated the nation's first president, Konstantin Päts, until the Soviet invasion in June 1940. Throughout most of the occupation period, the building was the office of the Supreme Soviet of the Estonian SSR, but after independence in 1991 it reverted to its original function. At the structure's rear is the presidential rose garden, which shares its back wall with that of the Kadriorg Palace's own manicured yard.

Due to their official function, the palace and garden are off limits to the public, but feel free to stroll in front of the palace to take a photograph or two. Here you can usually see two members of the president's honour guard standing to attention on either side of the main doors. They're part of the security battalion stationed at the building, and march out to change position – with stiff meticulousness – every two hours on even hours.

Above right: the hi-tech architecture of the KUMU
Right: classics of Estonian art on the third floor of the KUMU

Peter the Great's Cottage

At the end of the street, take a short walk to the left to reach the small **Peter the Great's Cottage** (Peter I Majamuuseum; Mäekalda 2; open May–Aug Wed–Sun 11am–7pm, Sept–Apr Wed–Sun 11am–4pm; admission charge). On the tsar's many visits to Tallinn during the construction of Kadriorg Palace, this tiny, simple cottage was his chosen abode. Its humble minimalism stands in sharp contrast to the baroque lavishness of the palace itself. Now a museum, it's decorated with period-appropriate furniture and displays a few of the emperor's personal belongings.

The KUMU

By this point, it's likely that you've already spotted the gigantic, futuristic-looking complex on the hillside to the right of Weizenbergi. It clearly stands out as something far larger, and more modern, than anything else in the vicinity. This is the KUMU (open May–Sept Tues–Sun 11am–6pm, Oct–Apr Wed–Sun 11am–6pm; admission charge), the new main building of the Art Museum of Estonia, and by far the largest art museum in the nation.

The KUMU, which derives its name from a contraction of the Estonian word 'kunstimuuseum' (art museum), opened its doors in early 2006. It differs from the art museums seen earlier on this tour as it concentrates specifically on Estonian art. Exposition space here is divided chronologically; the third floor is dedicated to the 'Classics of Estonian Art' from the 18th century to World War II, the fourth floor displays creations from the Soviet period, and the fifth floor exhibits contemporary works.

The museum's curators recommend allowing about 90 minutes to see the artworks, but you may also want to spend some time getting a good look at the building itself. The seven-storey structure was designed by Finnish archi-

tect Pekka Vapaavouri, and, in addition to the exhibition halls, has lecture halls, workshop rooms, an outdoor amphitheatre and a terrace café.

Russalka Memorial

After leaving the KUMU, head downhill and turn right, crossing in front of the Kadriorg Palace. Here you'll see a straight path, lined with benches, that leads towards the seashore. Once you pass the palace, you can head off this path to the right to explore some trails in the larger, more secluded area of Kadriorg Park. If you instead veer off to the left, you'll find monuments honouring two of Estonia's most prolific sculptors, Jaan Koort (1883–1935) and Amadus Adamson (1855–1929).

It was Adamson who created the magnificent figure that you'll reach at the end of this path, a statue of an angel, standing on a stone pedestal and facing out to sea. This dramatic monument is the **Russalka Memorial**, commemorating the 177 men lost when the Russian warship, *Russalka,* sank en route from Tallinn to Helsinki in 1893. Its wreck was assumed to be lost forever, but in 2003 a team of Estonian maritime researchers discovered it on the bottom of the sea, about 40km (25 miles) south of the Finnish capital. If you're here at the Russalka on a weekend, you may see Russian wedding couples stopping to fulfil their tradition of laying flowers.

From here, you can continue your stroll to the right along the shoreline path, cross back over the street to see Tallinn's Song Festival Grounds, birthplace of Estonia's 'Singing Revolution' *(see page 16)*, or head in the opposite direction along Narva Street to catch a bus or a taxi back to the centre.

5. OLD TOWN WALLS AND TOWERS *(see map pages 18–19)*

This half-day stroll takes you through the most intriguing and picturesque sections of the walls and towers that surround Tallinn's Old Town. You'll pass the massive Kiek in de Kök cannon tower and the scenic remnants of the old moat, then head into part of the wall itself.

Start by climbing the steps of Lühike jalg to reach a sheltered courtyard at its top. This is the **Danish King's Garden** (Taani kuninga aed), site of the first successful foreign invasion of Tallinn and, interestingly enough, the legendary birthplace of the Danish flag. It was on this spot that Danish King Valdemar II's troops were camped in 1219 when they battled to capture the Estonians' fortress on the hill. According to

Above: the Russalka Memorial
Right: taking a stroll in the Old Town

the tale, the Danes were losing the fight when suddenly the heavens opened up and a red flag with a white cross floated downward to them. Taking the event as a sign from God, the Danes were spurred on to victory. Historians believe that their decisive turnaround had more to do with a group of Slavic mercenaries who began attacking from the other side of the hill, but in any case, the red-and-white *Dannebrog* remains Denmark's flag to this day. To snap a photographic reference for this story, take a few steps down into the courtyard where you'll find a shield and sword decorated with the flag design.

If you're thinking about meals or a coffee at this point, note that the Vana Villemi Napsikamber pub, with its quiet terrace overlooking the courtyard, is the last decent place to eat along this route. Its entrance is at Lühike 9.

While deciding your meal plans, you can study the two towers here: the small, round **Stable Tower** (Tallitorn), and the larger, square **Virgins' Tower** (Neitsitorn), both dating to the 14th century. The name 'Virgins' Tower' is a bit of medieval irony – the building doubled as a prison for prostitutes.

Kiek in de Kök

Pass through the rectangular opening in the wall next to the Tallitorn, then head left through the park to reach the enormous **Kiek in de Kök** tower, once considered to be the most powerful cannon tower in the Baltic area. Its name in Low German literally means 'Peek into the Kitchen', a joking reference to the tower's dizzying 38-m (118-ft) height. Soldiers posted here claimed that from its top they could look straight down chimneys and see into neighbours' kitchens below.

Originally built in 1475–76, Kiek in de Kök was soon expanded to give it four storeys and walls that were 4m (13ft) thick. The enlargement proved a wise investment – when Ivan the Terrible laid siege to Tallinn during the Livonian War (1558–83), the tower, and hence the town, held up, though Ivan still managed to blow a hole in the tower's top storey that was reportedly big enough to drive two oxen through. During post-war repairs, builders set a row of stone cannon balls into the wall to commemorate the event. These can still be seen on the tower's southeast side.

Above: the Old Town's walls and towers, highlight of this tour

The tower now houses a **museum** (open Mar–Oct daily 10.30am–6pm; Nov–Feb daily 10.30am–5pm; admission charge) chronicling the history of the town's defences from the 13th to 18th centuries. Though the displays are dusty and dated, a visit will give you a chance to explore the tower's interior, see the views from its upper windows, and learn how the town's walls and towers developed.

That story began back in 1265, when Tallinn was first enclosed by stone barricades. The wall system we now see, however, started to take shape during a major expansion in the 14th century. Years of gradual repairs and improvement followed, and by its heyday in the 16th century, the wall was 2.4km (1 mile) long, 14–16m (46–52ft) high, about 3m (10ft) thick and included a total of 46 towers. Today, 1.9km (1½ miles) of the wall are still standing, along with 20 defence towers, two inner gate towers and sections of two outer gate towers.

Tunnels and Toompea Castle

Leaving the museum, as you're walking up Komandandi tee and down Falgi tee, **Deer Park** (Hirvepark) is below on your left. Though it's hard to see from this angle, you're standing on a stone-reinforced bastion. Curiously, a 17th-century system of **tunnels** runs along the bastion's base. In a bizarre historic twist, it was converted in Soviet times for use as a bomb shelter. In 2003, construction workers digging the foundation for the nearby Occupation Museum discovered a second tunnel system, also from the 17th century. Buried 8–9m (26–29ft) under the park and 225m (720ft) long, the 'new' passage is shaped like an irregular pentagon. Both tunnel systems were evidently designed to ferry powder to forward guards during an attack.

Now you pass the Old Town's best-protected building, **Toompea Castle**, on your right. After snapping a few obligatory photos of Tall Hermann (Pikk Hermann), a tower that is a powerful symbol of Estonian statehood,

Above: Schnelli Pond

take a quick detour underneath its base to get an idea of just how imposing the fortress would look from an enemy's perspective. Here the strategic advantage of its hilltop location becomes abundantly clear.

A Walk in the Park

Even better views of Toompea's limestone cliffs can be had from **Toompark**, one of Tallinn's most relaxing places to stroll. The W-shaped **Schnelli Pond** that runs through it was once part of the town's moat. Now it's a peaceful spot where locals feed ducks in summer and practise ice hockey in winter.

After crossing Nunne Street, you'll come to the most visible and accessible stretch of Tallinn's **town wall**. Once inside the large archway on Suur-Kloostri, turn right to enter the section of the wall that's open to the public (open Apr–May, Sept Mon–Wed, Fri noon–6pm, Sat–Sun 11am–4pm; June–Aug Mon–Fri 11am–7pm, Sat–Sun 11am–4pm; Oct–Mar Mon, Tues, Fri noon–5pm, Sat–Sun 11am–4pm; admission charge). The walkway along the top of the wall connects three towers: **Nun Tower** (Nunnatorn), **Sauna Tower** (Saunatorn) and **Golden Leg Tower** (Kuldjala torn). While up here, be sure to check out the medieval toilet, which posed an obvious hazard for anyone passing below.

The route through the park continues past several more towers. These are, in order: **Behind-the-Nuns** (Nunnedetagune), **Loewenschede**, **Rope Hill** (Kõismae), **Plate**, **Eppingi** and **Behind Grusbeke** (Grusbeke-tagune). All date back to the late 1300s and early 1400s.

Back to Pikk and the Old Town

Re-entering the town via Suurtüki brings you to one of the most curious streets in the Old Town, **Laboratooriumi**, which cuts along the inside of the town wall from this point. Among the strange buildings found on this street is a Ukrainian church with impossibly tiny windows, and a slot where you can drop requests for prayer. Laboratooriumi ends at a squat, round building that served as a horse mill from the 14th to the 18th centuries.

From here, it's just a short walk to Pikk Street, and the **Great Coast Gate** (Suur Rannavürav), one of Tallinn's two remaining outer gates. This is also the site of the mighty cannon tower known as **Fat Margaret** (Paks Margareeta). Details of these buildings are given in route 2 *(see pages 30–31)*, but a look at the inside of the tower that protected Tallinn from attacks by sea would be an appropriate finish to a tour of the town's defences.

Following Pikk in the opposite direction will bring you back to the centre of the Old Town, where opportunities for dining, shopping and more sightseeing are plentiful.

Right: Fat Margaret

6. PIRITA *(see map below)*

Spend two hours touring the majestic ruins of the 15th-century Pirita Convent, the Pirita River and Tallinn's most popular beach. Weather permitting, you can bring along your swimming kit and make a day of it.

Take buses 1A, 8, 34A or 38 from the Viru Centre's underground terminal to the Pirita stop.

Buses to Pirita conveniently stop in front of the area's most spectacular and historic sight, the ruins of **Pirita Convent** (Pirita klooster; open June–Aug daily 9am–6pm; Apr–May, Sept daily 10am–6pm; Oct–Mar daily noon–4pm; admission charge), which tower through the trees just east of the road. St Bridget's Convent, as it's more properly known, was founded in 1407 as part of a Swedish religious order, and was the largest convent in the Livonian territories. It operated until 1577 when it was destroyed by the forces of Ivan the Terrible, after which stones from the ruined buildings were immediately carted off for use in other construction projects in Tallinn. What remains of the original convent today are its 35-m (115-ft) gabled Gothic façade, the walls of its main building, and several foundations and cellars. The ruins now serve as a popular curiosity for tourists as well as a unique summer concert venue.

Once you enter the grounds, look at the diagram on the back of your ticket to find the location of the convent's various chambers and divisions, which you can trace as you make your way through its many still-visible

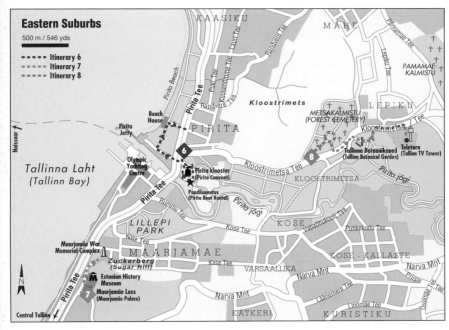

corridors and staircases. From the back of the ruins, you can also get some fairly good views of the nearby tributaries of the Pirita River, and you'll be able to spot the modern tower of the Bridgettine Convent, built in the post-Soviet period, when the order re-established its presence here.

Pirita River

The small road that leads downhill from just outside the convent's gates takes you to the edge of the Pirita River, which slowly winds its way through this valley before emptying out into Tallinn Bay. The rowing boats and canoes docked here are available for rental by the hour from the **Pirita Boat Rental** (Paadilaenutus; open May–Sept 10am–10pm), based in a shack to your left. An hour or two of lazily rowing through the marshy channels of the river will give you unforgettable views of the convent ruins.

The square building next to you on the riverbank provides a convenient opportunity for a lunch stop. Its main occupant is the Charital restaurant, which is far too formal for a daytime meal, but its Café Bellevue, upstairs, is decent and offers a panoramic view of the area.

Olympic Yachts and Pirita Beach

As you make your way across the wide, Merivülja Road and head towards the seashore, you can see the Pirita Harbour and imposing **Olympic Yachting Centre** across the mouth of the river to your left. The Yachting Centre was built for the 1980 Moscow Olympic Games, whose sailing events were held in Tallinn, prompting a local construction boom. In front, you'll see a long, concrete **jetty** that protects the harbour. Though it's something of a walk, you can make your way to its tip for a sailor's look at Tallinn's port and Old Town, and in doing so get a good dose of sea air.

The long, wide stretch of sand next to you is Pirita Beach. As Tallinn's most popular bit of coast, it's guaranteed to be packed with bronzing bodies on any hot summer weekend. To head along the beach to the north, you can either trudge straight across the sand, or use any of the pathways through the pine forest that backs up to the beach. The large, industrial-looking **beach house** here was also an Olympic addition. Its subsequent commercial success has been mediocre, as you can see by its many darkened windows, but it does offer a bowling club and a couple of snack bars.

Amenities on the beach itself include changing booths, volleyball courts and other conveniences for those who want to spend the day on the sand. You may find swimming here somewhat difficult, as the water is so shallow that you have to walk out quite a way from the shore before you're even up to your waist. On the other hand, the shallowness of the bay keeps the water warm.

From the car park behind the beach house, you can take one of the taxis that sometimes wait here, or head to the main road to catch a bus back to town.

Above left: Pirita Convent
Right: boats on the Pirita River

7. MAARJAMÄE *(see map page 48)*

See unforgettable relics of Estonia's World War II and Soviet periods on this compact, two- to three-hour outing to Maarjamäe Palace and the Maarjamäe War Memorial complex.

Take bus No. 5 from Viru Square to the Maarjamägi stop.

Your destination is Maarjamäe, a small, seaside hill along the Pirita Road, just north of the city centre. Once off the bus, make your way up the nearby set of steps to reach the grounds of the stately, pseudo-gothic **Maarjamäe Loss** (Maarjamäe Palace) at the top of the hill.

Maarjamäe Palace

The collection of buildings here, and the land that surrounds them, have a long and eclectic history. First mentioned as a summer estate as far back as the 17th century, the hill was originally called Streitberg or 'the Hill of Strife' because of its connection to a Livonian War battle. In 1811, a businessman named Clementz bought the property and established a sugar mill here, prompting the hill to be renamed Zuckerberg (Sugar Hill). Some of the small, stone buildings opposite the palace's main entrance date from that time. But the enterprise wasn't successful, nor were the starch factory, distillery and steam plant that his successor attempted.

In 1873, Anatoli Orlov-Davydov, a count from St Petersburg, bought the land to use as a summer residence. In honour of either his wife or

daughter (both were named Maria), he dubbed the estate Marienberg , from which the Estonian 'Maarjamäe' is derived. In 1874 he completed the grand house, with its octagonal tower and staircase leading down to the sea.

Through the subsequent decades, the Orlov-Davydovs made regular summer visits, often bringing along members of the tsar's family and other members of St Petersburg society. In the 1920s, however, they emigrated to France, and rented out the mansion to the Dutch consol to Estonia. From 1932 the palace was home to a popular restaurant-hotel, and later an all-night cabaret club. Its wilder days ended in 1937 when it became Estonia's military flight school, and after the Soviet invasion of 1940, it was nationalised and used as a barracks for Red Army officers.

In 1975 the palace was given over to the **Estonian History Museum** (open Mar–Oct Wed–Sun 11am–6pm; Nov–Feb Wed–Sun 10am–5pm; admission charge), and this branch *(see also page 28)* houses exhibitions on 19th- and 20th-century developments. Here you'll find excellent displays detailing the nation's War for Independence and the years of the first Estonian Republic. The most fascinating section of the museum may be its collection of World War II pho-

Above: commemorative stones at the Maarjamäe War Memorial complex

tographs, documents, uniforms and weapons. While not as extensive as those in equivalent museums in Western Europe, these displays provide insight into how that chapter of Europe's history played out in Estonia.

The post-war period is covered minimally in this museum (the exhibition actually ends with the 1950s), but there are a few Soviet-era curiosities to look for. One is the reproduction of a portable hut used by the Forest Brothers, Estonian resistance fighters who took to the woods in an attempt to drive out Soviet forces. Another is the enormous, propagandistic mural, painted by Evald Okas, which combines images of happy workers, cosmonauts, wheat fields, and countless other staples of socialist symbolism. You may have to make a special request to see it.

One sight that's not to be missed is the collection of imposing statues – Lenin, Stalin, Kalinin and other fallen Soviet heroes – removed from their places of prominence around the country and now lying in a stack behind the palace while the museum figures out what to do with them. In this seemingly abandoned state, they certainly create a powerful image of the fall of the USSR.

War Memorial

Next to the museum grounds, a short walk from the bottom of the stairs, stands Tallinn's largest and most surreal Soviet-era monument, the sprawling **Maarjamäe War Memorial complex**. With its huge, grass-covered earthworks, concrete slab avenues, abstract sculptures and eternal flame, it shares a similar pomp and grandiosity with other World War II memorials built all across the USSR in the 1960s and '70s. Although some of its elements, such as the obelisk (1960), are older, the bulk of the complex was created in 1975. As you explore, you'll find a row of pedestals bearing inscriptions honouring various military units, as well as an amphitheatre that was used for Communist youth rallies. Sadly, the complex has now fallen into disrepair, neglected by everyone except skateboarders and graffiti artists.

As unlikely as this story already sounds, the triplet crosses visible behind the complex reveal an even stranger truth about the site: it's actually a German war cemetery. Underneath this hill are the remains of over 1.700 Nazi troops killed as Germany was pushing the Red Army out of Estonia in 1941. After the war, the Soviets bulldozed the area and built their victory monument on top of it. In 1998, a German veterans' group funded the partial restoration of the cemetery. Now, after more than 50 years, soldiers of both armies are honoured here side by side.

Above and right: hand sculpture and crosses at the Maarjamäe War Memorial complex

8. KLOOSTRIMETSA *(see map page 48)*

This half-day trip to the serene Kloostrimetsa area takes in the Forest Cemetery, Tallinn Botanic Garden and the city's TV Tower, the tallest building in Estonia.

Take bus 34A or 38 from the Viru Centre's underground terminal to the Metsakalmistu stop. This route works best either late morning or early afternoon.

Just as its name implies, Kloostrimetsa (literally 'Convent's Forest') is a densely wooded area just beyond the Pirita River and the 15th-century Pirita Convent *(see page 48)*. Though it's well within the city limits, it has the quiet, pleasantly secluded feel of a place that is much further from civilisation.

VIP Cemetery

Once you arrive at the bus stop, cross the road to reach the extensive **Forest Cemetery** (Metsakalmistu), where Estonia buries its dead – or at least its most respected dead. Since its establishment in 1933, this has been Estonia's VIP cemetery, the final resting place of politicians, poets, actors and other public personae. The cemetery is in fact organised according to their various spheres of activity, with separate sections allotted to sports figures, writers, doctors, artists, war veterans, etc. At its gates you'll find a plan, in Estonian, showing the cemetery's layout and detailing where the various plots are located. The diagram also points out the graves of the more famous historical and cultural figures.

You can take your time exploring the cemetery, reading the headstones and visiting the functionalist, limestone chapel, which dates to 1936. Alter-

Above: view over Kloostrimetsa, showing the Botanic Garden and TV Tower

natively, you can head straight to the cemetery's most interesting area, where several key luminaries are buried. The diagram will help you find the short path, parallel to the road, next to which lie the likes of the matriarch of Estonian poetry, Lydia Koidula (1843–86), chess champion Paul Keres (1916–75) and singer Georg Ots (1920–75). At the end of this row you'll find the graves of Estonia's first president Konstantin Päts (1874–1956) and his family, their fairly plain tombstones displaying a typically Estonian modesty.

Tallinn Botanic Garden

After leaving the nearby gate, continue up the road a few paces, then look for a drive leading off to your right. It ends at the modern pavilion of the **Tallinn Botanic Garden** (Tallinna Botaanikaaed; houses open daily 11am–4pm, garden open daily 11am–7pm; admission charge). From here, follow the signs directing you to the 'Sissepüüs' (entrance), around the other side.

    With over 4,500 plant species on display, the garden has enough variety in its collection to keep any botanist in awe for days. You don't have to know the names of a single flower or tree though to appreciate the earthy beauty of the lush greenhouses, open year-round. In summer, the most popular attraction here is the extensive rose garden, but you can also wander the rest of the 123-hectare (304-acre) grounds, visiting the arboretum, lilac garden and areas dedicated to perennials, annuals, bulbous plants, etc.

TV Tower

From nearly everywhere in the garden, the soaring **Tallinn TV Tower** (Tallinna Teletorn, open daily 10am–midnight; admission charge) is plainly visible. To reach it, make your way up the long set of wooden stairs across from the Botanic Garden's main doors, cross the car park, then carefully head right, along the shoulder of the road.

    Built in 1980 – not coincidentally the same year Tallinn hosted the yachting events of the summer Olympics – the imposing 314-m (1,030-ft) concrete tower is Estonia's tallest building by far. Visitors can take the lift to its round observation deck at the 170-m (558-ft) level, from where the coast of Finland is said to be visible on a clear day. No matter how the skies look though, a trip here is definitely worth the cost of the ticket, if only to see the spectacular view of the nearby forest and coast, not to mention the tower's own gargantuan structure and tacky interior design, unchanged since the late Soviet period. The restaurant that operates here, when not reserved for wedding parties, is a fun place to stay for lunch or drinks, and is an especially romantic spot at sunset.

    Once you've cured yourself of vertigo, you can cross the road to catch the bus back to the centre.

Right: the TV Tower up close

9. ESTONIAN OPEN AIR MUSEUM *(see map below)*

Experience Estonia's rural past by touring this elaborate museum.

Taxi is the recommended way to reach the museum, but you can also take bus 21 from the train station to the Rocca al Mare stop.

By and large, Estonia is a nation that remains very much connected to its rural roots; where many college students spend weekends in the fields helping their grandparents gather apples and potatoes, and where just about everything that's considered 'typically Estonian' comes straight out of a village cookbook.

It's precisely this rustic heritage that is the focus of the **Estonian Open Air Museum** (Eesti Vabaõhumuuseum; Vabaõhumuuseumi tee 12; open May–Sept daily 10am–8pm; Oct–Apr daily 10am–5pm; admission charge), a vast, seaside park at the northwest edge of town. Originally a summer estate with the romantic name of Rocca al Mare ('Rock by the Sea' in Italian), the 79-hectare (195-acre) wooded area is now a 'living museum', home to a large collection of 18th- to 20th-century thatched farm buildings, windmills, watermills, and other village structures – more than 70 buildings in all. Rather than simply being part of a static display, the buildings here are carefully positioned and furnished, many of them staffed by employees dressed in period costume who demonstrate various traditional

Estonian Open Air Museum

400 m / 437 yds

····· Itinerary 9

Fishermans Huts

Netsheds

Tallinna Laht (Tallinn Bay)

Rusi Talu (Rusi Farm)
Jüri-Jaagu Talu (Jüri-Jaagu Farm)
Roosta Talu (Roosta Farm)
Kahala Vesiveski (Kahala Watermill)
Kolga Talu (Kolga Farm)
Kalma Tuulik (Kalma Windmill)
Kerase Talu (Kerase Farm)
Orametsa Pritsikuur (Orametsa Fire Station)
Sutlepa Kabel (Sutlepa Chapel)
Kuie Koolimaja (Kuie Village School)
Nütsi Tuulik (Nütsi Windmill)
Kalu Körts (Kalu Tavern)
Kutsari-Hürjapea Talu (Kutsari-Hürjapea Farm)
Sepa Talu (Sepa Farm)
Sassi-Jaani Talu (Sassi-Jaani Farm)
Polga Talu (Polga Farm)
Nuki Talu (Nuki Cotter's Dwelling Farm)
ÕISMÄE
EESTI VABAÕHUMUUSEUM (ESTONIAN OPEN AIR MUSEUM)
ROCCA AL MARE
Rocca al Mare Bus Stop
Vabaõhumuuseumi Tee
Vabaõhumuuseumi Tee
Halli Tee
Tädra Tee
Lea Tee
Tamula Tee
Lõuka Tee
Rannamõisa Tee
HAABERSTI
Central Tallinn
Zoo, Rocca al Mare Tivoli

Above: house interior
Right: weaving handicrafts

activities, all the while telling visitors what the various structures and implements were used for.

There are several ways to tour the park. The most common is to explore it by foot, reading informational signs and asking the staff questions as you go. Other options include renting a bicycle, which you can do for a very reasonable fee. or paying for an audioguide, an electronic device that provides a detailed narrative about each of the museum's major sights.

The farms and other buildings are grouped into four zones, reflecting the various regions of Estonia – North Estonia, South Estonia, West Estonia and the islands. There's no obvious single route that will cover all the sights without backtracking, but generally you can start by going straight from the entrance. and then making an anti-clockwise circle through the area.

Estonian Farmstead and Traditional Tavern

After entering, you'll see the long, threshing-barn-house of the **Sassi-Jaani Farm** ahead on your left. This is a typical Western Estonian farmstead from the late 18th-/ early-19th century. Such a farm would have cultivated about 50 hectares (123 acres), and its household would have had 15 to 18 people. In its yard are a storehouse, cattle shed, summer kitchen and a well. Here, as with all the other farms and buildings, you're free to drop in and take a look around.

Further along is the lively **Kolu Tavern** (Kolu Körts), which offers your only opportunity to eat in the museum (unless you brought a picnic lunch). Dating to 1840, the tavern represents what would have been a hub of social and business activity in any 19th-century village. In front of the tavern there's usually a horse carriage and driver, which you can hire for a ride through the park. If you do stop here, try the tavern's traditional pea soup.

Windmills and Swings

From this part of the road you can already see the sturdy, two-storey **Nütsi Windmill**, which makes an excellent photograph, positioned as it is in a sunny clearing with the sea at its back. Post windmills such as this were used to perform the all-important task of grinding flour, and each would typically serve several villages. Its sails would be covered in cloth, the long pole at its back could be used to pivot the entire apparatus around its post/shaft, turning it to catch the wind.

At this point, you may want to swing back to the right to cover some of the areas you passed. These include the **Pulga Farm** with its limestone

buildings, the relatively affluent, 1930s-era **Kutsari-Hürjapea Farm**, and the **Nuki Cotter's Dwelling**, where the poorest kind of peasants lived.

If instead you continue left towards the sea, you pass a **village swing** – a focal point of social activity in any rural Estonian community – and come to a cluster of farms surrounded by low, rock walls. These are the **Roosta Farm**, the **Jüri-Jaagu Farm**, and the **Kolga Farm**, representing Estonia's largest islands, Saaremaa, Hiiumaa and Muhu, respectively. Note the prayer house at the edge of the Roosta Farm, and be sure to drop into the Jüri-Jaagu Farm to see the colourful, woven textiles created by island women.

Along the shore you'll see some **net sheds** and a **fisherman's hut** and, if you turn back towards the land, a row of **island windmills** along a low ridge.

Final Attractions

As you begin to circle back toward the museum's entrance, follow the path that cuts through the middle of the park. This will take you past the **Kahala Watermill**, the early-20th-century **Orgmetsa Fire Station** and close to the **Sutlepa Chapel**. Dating to 1699, this working chapel is the oldest building in the museum and is representative of the nation's many ethnic Swedish communities, whose ancestors settled along Estonia's islands and coasts in the 13th century.

One essential building, and a relatively new addition to the museum, is the nearby **Kuie Village School**, which dates to 1878. Inside are the schoolmaster's living quarters and a large classroom, where programmes are held for children.

Above: farm buildings
Left: traditional crafts

Back to Tallinn

Leaving the museum, you can either catch a bus or order a taxi to take you back into town. If you're travelling with children, you may want to visit other attractions in this part of town before heading too far. These include **Tallinn Zoo** (Paldiski mnt. 145; open daily May–Aug 9am–7pm; Mar–Apr and Sept–Oct 9am–5pm; Nov–Feb 9am–3pm; admission charge), and the **Rocca al Mare Tivoli** (Paldiski mnt. 100; open mid-May–Aug Mon–Fri noon–8pm, Sat–Sun 11am–8pm), the city's largest amusement park.

10. SOVIET SIGHTS *(see map pages 18–19)*

The tragedies and controversies surrounding Estonia's Soviet past come to light on this brief visit to the Linda Monument, the Museum of Occupations and the Bronze Soldier.

Without a doubt, the most sensitive subject in today's Estonia is the nation's forced annexation into the USSR during World War II and the half-century of Soviet occupation that followed. This is a deeply emotional issue that continues to cause tensions between Estonia and its largest neighbour, Russia, with each side interpreting the events of those years in very different ways. One view, hardened by decades of official Soviet propaganda, claims that the USSR's 1944 invasion 'liberated' Estonia from the Nazis and reinstated its 'voluntary' membership in the Soviet Union. For most Estonians, however, the Soviet reinvasion at the end of the war simply replaced one repressive totalitarian regime with another – one that effectively destroyed their independent state, caused immeasurable suffering and left them trapped for decades on the wrong side of the Iron Curtain. It's fair to say that this prickly question has complicated the relationship between Estonians and the sizable ethnic Russian minority living here, families of those relocated to Estonia by the thousands during the Soviet period. Many years after independence, this group is still struggling to find its place in the new republic.

Linda Monument

Our tour commences at **Linda's Hill** (Lindamügi), a tiny, park area just beside Falgi tee, directly across from Toompea Castle. Follow any path to the top of the hill to reach the park's central feature, the solemn statue of a weeping woman. This is the **Linda Monument**, created by the renowned Tallinn sculptor Amandus Adamson in 1920.

Right: Linda Monument

The work shows Tallinn's mythical matriarch Linda grieving the death of her husband, Kalev. It was probably thanks to the statue's seemingly benign, folkloric subject that it wasn't destroyed by the Soviet regime as were so many of Tallinn's other pre-war monuments. In Soviet times, however, the sculpture took on a new meaning, as locals began to use it as an unsanctioned memorial to loved ones who had been sent to Siberia, particularly those who suffered during the infamous mass deportations of 1941 and 1949. In those two events, a total of over 30,000 Estonians, mainly women and children, were arrested, loaded onto boxcars and sent east. Because there were no gravesites and no official memorials to these victims, many Tallinners would honour their relatives by laying flowers at the Linda Monument, an act of defiance that could earn them a jail sentence if caught.

Today locals continue to bring flowers to the site, which has become widely recognised as a symbol of national grief for the victims of Soviet repression. The plaque at the statue's base reads, 'Still thinking of those who were taken from here, their angst cries to heaven.'

Symbols of Power

Returning to Falgi tee, you'll see two emblems of Estonia's Soviet-era independence movement. The most obvious is **Tall Hermann** (Pikk Hermann), a tower on Toompea castle above you. For centuries, it has been a widely accepted tenet that whichever nation flies its flag on Tall Hermann can claim to be the true ruler of Estonia. So when, on 24 February 1989 (the 71st anniversary of the Estonian Republic), the banned Estonian tricolour appeared on the tower instead of the Soviet red and yellow, it was a major victory for the cause and sparked mass demonstrations. The other symbol of those times is the **boulder** at the corner of Falgi tee and Toompea. Bearing the date of Estonia's re-established independence, 20 August 1991, it's a souvenir of those chaotic August days when Tallinners erected stone barricades here to keep Soviet tanks from rolling onto the hill.

Museum of Occupations

From that corner, head to the bottom of Toompea Street and turn right to find the **Museum of Occupations** (open Tues–Sun 11am–6pm; admission charge), a very modern presentation of the nation's 1940–91 period. Though the museum takes a decidedly nationalistic and emotional standpoint, with

Above: Toompea Castle's Tall Hermann
Right: commemorating Independence Day in Tallinn

rows of tattered suitcases in the hall serving as a reminder of how the deportations affected so many ordinary people, it will give you a fairly complete picture of that segment of Estonian history. The museum not only deals with the hardships caused by both the Nazi and Soviet regimes, it also shows ordinary life during the relatively calm, post-Stalin decades.

If you need a break from all this weighty, historic reflection, note that the museum also houses a fairly decent café. You may also want to visit the building's basement level to see the discarded statues of some of Estonia's Communist-era heroes.

Bronze Soldier

After leaving the museum, carefully cross the wide, divided Karli pst., then head right to reach the so-called **Bronze Soldier**, central Tallinn's most prominent – and controversial – Soviet war memorial. This striking figure of a mourning soldier against a white, brick wall was installed in 1947 as a kind of 'tomb of the unknown soldier', and in Soviet times had a gas-fuelled 'eternal flame' burning at its base.

Since the collapse of Soviet power, there has been talk of getting rid of the Bronze Soldier, or at least moving it to a less central location. So far though, the only changes made to it have been the extinguishing of the gas flame and revision of the text to read simply 'For those fallen in World War II' without reference to either side. Given the Bronze Soldier's history though, it's not surprising that many Estonians still find the presence of such a monument in downtown Tallinn offensive, particularly each May 9, when hundreds of Soviet Army veterans gather here to celebrate the USSR's victory in the 'Great Patriotic War'. For ordinary Russians though, it would be a crime to remove the monument as they, like those who visit the Linda Monument, continue to lay flowers here in memory of relatives who never returned.

excursions

Excursions

1. HELSINKI *(see pullout map and page 62)*

Finland's bustling capital, just 85km (52 miles) across the gulf, makes an excellent day trip from Tallinn.

Nordic Jet Line and Silja Line ships from Tallinn's Passenger Port and Lindaline ships from the Linnahall harbour take you directly into central Helsinki in under two hours. Try to pick up one of the free maps available on board or at the ferry terminal. Another option is to take the helicopter from Tallinn (see page 83 for details). Note that this day trip works best in the warmer months, when these fast ferries operate.

Coming from Tallinn, Helsinki will strike you as affluent, modern and booming. When Swedish King Gustav I founded the city in 1550, his aim was in fact to rival its thriving Hanseatic neighbour to the south. Helsinki only came into its own after 1812, when Russia, having taken over the Finnish territory from the Swedes, moved the capital here from Turku. The tsarist era brought with it the grand, neoclassical architecture that's still the city centre's trademark, though constant development since Finland's 1917 independence has added other styles to the mix. Thanks to fast-paced building in the 1980s and '90s and the energy of the Finns, the city now has a cutting-edge yet orderly feel.

Main Attractions

Once you disembark at the harbour, make your way to the busy, colourful harbour market, the **Kauppatori**, where everything from fish to souvenirs is on sale. After perusing the T-shirts and eels, head one block north down Katariinankatu or Sofiankatu where you'll find Helsinki's main attraction, the **Senate Square** (Senaatintori). Towering above you is the white **Helsinki Cathedral** (open June–Aug daily 9am–midnight; Sept–May daily 9am–6pm; admission free). Also known as the Evangelical-Lutheran Cathedral, it was built from 1830–52 and is topped by 12 zinc statues representing the apostles. You'll find that its whitewashed interior, though impressive in scale, is remarkably plain.

The cathedral, square and two buildings flanking it were designed by Carl Ludvig Engel, a German architect who played a key role in the city's early 19th-century development. The empire-style he favoured can be seen in the Government Palace (1822) on the square's eastern side and the University (1832) opposite. In the centre of the square is a statue of Tsar Aleksander II.

Helsinki's other grand cathedral, which you can see east of the market, is the **Uspenski Cathedral**

Left: relaxing in Helsinki
Right: Eliel Saarinen's Helsinki Central Railway Station

(Kanavakatu 1; open May–Sept Mon–Fri 9.30am–4pm, Sat 9.30am–2pm, Sun noon–3pm; Oct–Apr Tues–Fri 9.30am–4pm, Sat 9.30am–2pm, Sun noon–3pm; admission free), said to be the largest Russian Orthodox cathedral in the West. Consecrated in 1868, the red-brick church has 13 gilded onion domes and is filled with a fabulous collection of icons.

Other Sights

From the market, take a leisurely stroll west down the park-like **Esplanadi**, one of the city centre's most popular beauty spots. At its end, on the right, you'll find the Stockmann department store, which is a retail Mecca and city landmark. Mannerhemintie, Helsinki's main boulevard, defines the area on Stockmann's opposite side. Any of the restaurants and cafés here will serve for a meal break, but for something different, try the tractor-themed Zetor pub (Mannerheimintie 3–5), on the right as you start up the street.

Mannerhemintie brings you to a large square on your right, home to **Helsinki Central Railway Station**, designed by architect Eliel Saarinen and inaugurated in 1919. This building, with its titanic statues and 48.5-m (159-ft) clock tower, makes a wonderful centrepiece to the downtown area. On the same square is the city's contemporary art museum, the **Kiasma** (Mannerheiminaukio 2; open Tues 9am–5pm, Wed–Sun 10am–8.30pm; admission charge).

After leaving the square, cross Mannerheimintie, head due west down Arkadiankatu and turn right on Fredrikinkatu. You should come to a small hill, inside which is the **Temppeliaukio Church** (open Mon, Wed 10am–5pm, Tues 10am–12.45pm, 2.15pm–5pm, Thur, Fri 10am–8pm, Sat 10am–

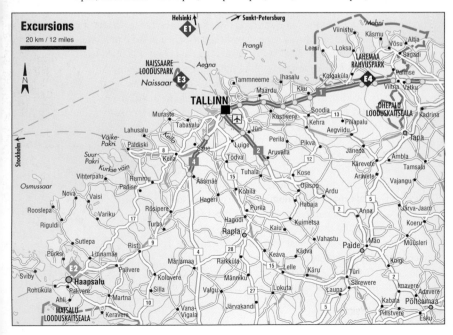

6pm, Sun 11.45am–1.45pm, 3.30–6pm; admission free). Hewn out of natural bedrock in 1969, the so-called 'Rock Church' has been likened to the set of a Bond film and is unrivalled in its weird modernity. Inside, its rust-red natural walls provide wonderful acoustics.

Tourist Tram

On nearby Runeberginkatu, to the west, you can hop on the **3T tram** (buy a ticket from the driver). This 'tourist tram' makes a one-hour trip through the city, giving you a look at the neighbourhoods around the centre. It takes you past the Olympic Stadium, built for the 1952 games, the Botanical Gardens and the Tivoli. You can leave the tram at any point to explore, or ride it to the harbour for your boat back to Tallinn.

2. HAAPSALU *(see map opposite)*

The relaxing, seaside resort town of Haapsalu is steeped in history and early-20th-century charm.

Frequent express buses depart from Tallinn's main bus station. The journey takes 1½–2 hours.

Nestled on Estonia's west coast 99km (62 miles) from Tallinn, Haapsalu has long attracted tourists of one sort or another. Since its founding in 1279, the town has been plundered by pirates, burned down by the Russians, sold to the Danes and captured by the Swedes. A more welcome sort of visitor began arriving when Dr Carl Abraham Hunnius, who had discovered the curative properties of the local sea mud, founded the first health resort here in 1825. Soon Haapsalu became a popular destination for St Petersburg aristocracy, and even Tchaikovsky came here to unwind. After some post-Soviet sprucing-up, this little city of 12,000 once again draws an international crowd with its spa resorts, beaches and old-fashioned wooden architecture.

Get off the bus at the first Haapsalu stop, a shopping centre on Tallinna mnt. At the large junction in front of you, turn right onto Posti, Haapsalu's main street. It's hard to get lost in this tiny town, but you can pick up a free map at the Tourist Information Centre, which you'll pass at Posti 37.

Episcopal Castle

A few minutes' walk down Posti will quickly bring you to Haapsalu's most fascinating historic feature, the ruin of the **Episcopal Castle**, which dominates the centre of town. Built in the 13th-century, the castle served as both a religious outpost and a military fortress until it was heavily damaged during the Livonian War (1558–83). Most of the remaining castle was pulled down on the orders of Peter the Great in the early 1700s, but the outer walls and part of the structure are still standing. You can stroll through

Above: central Helsinki
Right: the Episcopal Castle

its grassy courtyard and examine the cannons and remaining walls.

In summer, the castle's watchtower and a small museum are in operation (open Tues–Sun 10am–6pm; admission charge). A ticket to the museum lets you into the beautiful **Dome Church**, the only truly intact part of the castle. One of the church's windows is central to Haapsalu's famous 'Legend of the White Lady', which claims that the ghostly figure of a woman, who was immured in the castle walls, appears here on moonlit nights in August. The town holds its annual music festival, the White Lady Days, in honour of her arrival.

Outside the castle, across the parking area to the right, is the **Läänemaa Museum** (Kooli 2; open mid-May–mid-Sept Wed–Sun 10am–6pm; mid-Sept–mid-May Wed–Sun 11am–4pm; admission charge), which will give you an overview of the town's development.

Promenade and Peninsula

A few paces north brings you to the town's beloved seaside **Promenade**, an excellent place to stroll. On the left-hand side of the path is a fairly new, climbable **bird-watching tower**. The other direction takes you to the beautifully restored, 19th-century **Kuursaal** (Resort Hall), with its flowerbeds and bandstand. The Kuursaal is by far the town's most historic place to stop for lunch. Just beyond it is a talking and music-playing **stone bench** that serves as a monument to Tchaikovsky. The Russian composer spent the summer of 1867 in Haapsalu and, according to some, gained inspiration for *Swan Lake* by his stay.

From here, you can continue to explore the peninsula, or make your way back through the centre of town to the junction where you started. A turn right onto Jaama will take you to Haapsalu's pride and joy – the **Railway Station**, built in 1907 to accommodate visits by the tsar's family. Here the small **Estonian Railway Museum** (open Wed–Sun 10am–6pm; admission charge) presents the station's history. You can also wander the station's restored platform area and inspect the antique locomotives parked nearby.

Behind the station, footpaths lead west to Haapsalu's popular **Paralepa Beach** and the restaurant at the Fra Mare resort. Buses back to Tallinn leave from a stop directly in front of the railway station.

3. NAISSAAR   *(see map page 62)*

This forested island 10km (6 miles) off Tallinn's coast was a restricted military zone in Soviet times. Now a nature reserve, it's littered with rusting sea mines and other strange remnants of its military past.

On summer weekends, the M/S Monica *makes the voyage from Pirita Harbour. Contact the boat's operator (www.saartereisid.ee) for the latest timetable.*

Top: colourful Haapsalu rooftops. **Above:** buying fresh produce in Haapsalu
Right: the island of Naissar

Given Naissaar's predominantly male-centred military history, it's somewhat ironic that its name actually means 'women's island'. The title is thought to originate from an 11th-century legend about a race of beautiful maidens – and beastly men – who made their home here. Maidens or no maidens, the strategically-located island has had a military presence since 1730, when the first naval fortress was built here. Major development came in the 20th century, when the Russians used the island during both world wars. For the following fifty years, Naissaar remained a highly restricted Soviet naval base whose main function was the manufacture of sea mines, the casings of which still litter the island. When the Russians decommissioned the base in the early 1990s, they did a thorough job of defusing all their own mines, but the earlier wars had left other deadly souvenirs, including munitions and landmines, scattered throughout the forests. Before Naissaar could be opened to tourists in 1998, a de-mining operation removed over 5,000 of the explosive devices. However, many are still there, so it's *essential* that you stay on established trails.

Because of the island's size, 11km (7 miles) long and 4km (2½ miles) wide, and the fact that it's mostly untamed, exploring it is an involved process. Many visitors prefer to take the tour offered by Naissaare Reisid (tel: 639 8000; info@naissaarereisid.ee), which offers the only way to see Naissaar by car. Otherwise be prepared for a day of serious wilderness hiking or biking, and bring along adequate food, water and, critically, mosquito repellent.

Camping on the island is possible, as long as you register with the Nature Park Centre. Unless you plan to spend the night, be sure to carefully plan your hike so that you don't miss the afternoon boat back to the mainland.

Island Attractions

Once off the boat, head to the **Nature Park Centre**, just up the hill ahead of you. Here you'll find information, coffee, and maps of the island's two major trails. These will take you all around the island, its forests and its secluded, sandy beaches. Animals you might spot during your wanderings include deer, fox, rabbits and even moose. Keep an eye out for the beautiful, pink *Rosa Rugosa,* which blooms all over the island in summer.

A 20-minute walk from the port (follow the signs) brings you to the island's only village, **Männiku**, home to a pub, guesthouse and railway station. Here,

one enterprising local offers locomotive rides along a 2-km (1¼-mile) stretch of the old, narrow-gauge railway system that crosses the island.

Follow your trail map to find the island's most interesting military sights: the abandoned **mine factory**, the so-called **Fairy Village**, which is an eerie ghost town where Soviet military personnel lived, and **Bunker 10B**, the remains of a concrete bunker destroyed by retreating Russian soldiers in 1918. The trails will also bring you to the island's **lighthouses** and the **cemeteries** where British and French soldiers from the Crimean War were buried.

4. LAHEMAA NATIONAL PARK *(see map below)*

This road-trip through Estonia's largest national park takes in Palmse and Sagadi manor houses, seaside villages and Viinistu Art Museum.

For this excursion, you will need a car.

Lahemaa National Park covers a 725 square-km (280 square-mile) section of forests and coastline east of Tallinn. To reach it, head out of Tallinn on the Narva highway (E20). After about an hour you'll see the turn-off at Viitna, from where you should proceed north.

Manor Houses

The first stop on this tour is **Palmse Manor**, the most striking manor house in Estonia and Lahemaa's most popular attraction. The site of a 13th-century Cistercian nunnery, the land was purchased in 1673 by a family of Baltic German nobles, the Von der Pahlens. They constructed the house in 1730, rebuilding it in 1785. During the Soviet period the property was used as a Pioneer summer camp and fell into disrepair, but the house and grounds have now been restored.

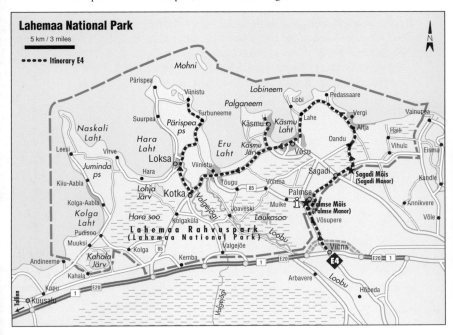

The main house, decorated with empire furniture, functions as a museum (open May–Sept daily 10am–7pm; Oct–Apr Mon–Fri 10am–3pm; admission charge). The manor's former distillery now operates as a boutique hotel, and one of the stables accommodates a small **museum** of antique carriages and automobiles (open in summer).

In one of the outbuildings is the **Lahemaa Visitors' Centre** (open May–Aug daily 9am–7pm; Sept–Apr Mon–Fri 9am–5pm). In here, pick up a detailed road map of Lahemaa, as the area's roads are poorly marked. The centre will also inform you about the park's nature trails and wildlife.

A few minutes northeast is **Sagadi**, Lahemaa's other prominent manor house, built in 1749 and renovated later that century. Like Palmse, its grounds are open to visitors. One of its outbuildings houses a forestry museum.

Altja, Käsmu and Viinistu

Continue northeast for **Altja**, a traditional fishing village restored in the 1970s and now a popular tourist spot. Visitors can try out its old swing and take the walk along the paths that lead to the seashore. Altja's tavern restaurant is a good place for lunch, but it gets crowded on summer weekends.

The coastal road west brings you to **Käsmu**, the 'Captains' Village', known for its picturesque homes. The town owes its wealth to smuggling. In the 19th century, salt was the hot commodity; in the days of Finland's dry laws in the 1920s and '30s, it was alcohol. After driving around to see the captains' houses, stop at the **Käsmu Maritime Museum** (open 24 hours; admission charge), in the former school of navigation.

Drive west to Loksa, then veer north to reach the tiny, coastal **Viinistu**. This village, with a population of about 150, offers a pleasant pub, a restaurant and paths along its rock-strewn shore. Its main attraction is the **Viinistu Art Museum** (open June–Sept daily 11am–6pm; Oct–May Wed–Sun 11am–6pm; admission charge), home to Estonia's largest private art collection. The museum, built in the remains of a Soviet-era fish factory, was created by one of Viinistu's native sons, who made his fortune as the manager of ABBA.

From here you can continue to drive around the loop of the peninsula, or return straight to Loksa, then head south to meet the highway back to Tallinn.

Above: Palmse Manor
Right: timber barn and meadow flowers, Viinistu

Leisure Activities

SHOPPING

Tallinn isn't the bargain paradise it was in the 1990s, but there are still enough tempting deals here – not to mention one-of-a-kind souvenir items – to keep a dedicated shopper busy for days. Thanks mostly to the tourism boom and a jump in the Estonians' own buying power, the eastern city centre and western portion of the Old Town have become solidly retail-focused over the last decade, which is all the more reason to keep an eye on the shop windows while you're out sightseeing.

What to Buy
Handicrafts

Various sorts of traditional, folk-inspired handicrafts *(käsitöö)* are by far the most popular and quintessentially Estonian of all souvenirs available. **Knitwear** leads the pack, especially hand-knitted jumpers, scarves, gloves and mittens created in uniquely Estonian/ Nordic patterns.

For something on the weird and whimsical side, look for knitted hats, including fabulously long, pointed caps that can also be wrapped around the neck to double up as scarves.

Linen is Estonia's other traditional textile. Though Western visitors mainly associate it with kitchen tablecloths, here it's used to make everything from men's shirts to baby clothes to curtains.

Apart from the unmistakable scent of wool, Tallinn's handicraft shops are filled with a distinctly sweet, dry fragrance that comes from another local material – **juniper wood**. Toys, beer mugs, sugar bowls, butter knives and other items carved from this (and sometimes pine) make inexpensive and lightweight gifts. Likewise, intricately made **leather** items – such as satchels and leather-bound notebooks – have a distinctly Estonian look and are easy to fit in a suitcase.

Left: traditional dress
Right: Baltic speciality

If you have a little more cash to spend and a passionate interest in traditional Estonian culture, note that the more serious handicraft shops sell complete women's **folk costumes**. These are famous for their vibrant, striped skirts that lend their colour to the nation's Song and Dance Festivals. A less extreme – and less costly – way to take home a folk costume is to buy one of the **dolls** that come in the same type of folk dress.

Amber

One souvenir that seems to be everywhere in Tallinn, but isn't Estonian at all, is **amber**. The material is actually imported from the Polish and Lithuanian coasts, but has become something of a pan-Baltic item. In addition to the rich, dark, whisky colour that people usually associate with it, amber also comes in white, gold, green and all shades of brown.

Ceramics

Beyond the traditional folk handicrafts, a few other hand-made creations have become mainstays of the souvenir-shop shelves. Painted **ceramics** are a popular choice. They come in the form of tiny, scale models of well-known Old Town build-

ings, some designed to be lit from the inside with a candle. Cups, plates and mugs featuring Tallinn skylines are also available. More artistically minded visitors should look for the wild ceramic creations sold in art shops.

Antiques

Shops across the Old Town sell **antiques** of all sorts, from gramophones to Russian icons. History buffs may want to pick up some of the World War II and Soviet-era relics available in these same shops. Propagandistic 'pins' and postcards from the 1980s cost only a few kroon.

Other Gifts

Among the other off-beat, artistic gifts typically sold here, brightly coloured, **hand-painted silk items**, such as scarves and neckties are popular, as are **quilts**, **stained-glass wares** and **hand-made jewellery**. Vodka drinkers may also consider picking up a set of **etched shot glasses**, available in souvenir motifs.

Souvenir shops also seem to do a good trade in **Russian nesting dolls**. These have absolutely nothing to do with Estonia, but picking up a set is a good way to trick your friends into thinking you made it all the way to Moscow.

Finally, it should be mentioned that, thanks to lower taxes, alcohol and cigarettes are relatively cheap in Estonia. The town's trademark tipple is the sweet **Vana Tallinn liqueur**, sold in special souvenir satchels.

Where to Shop

Without a doubt, the Old Town is Tallinn's most interesting shopping district. Not only does it have the highest concentration of souvenir shops, antiques shops, fashion boutiques and the like, but many of these are housed inside intriguing medieval buildings that a visitor wouldn't otherwise get to explore.

Above: local firewater, Vana Tallinn

The downside of Old Town shopping is that this is where herds of cruise ship passengers congregate, leading to price inflation. The shops furthest from Viru Street, Town Hall Square and the Toompea lookouts are likely to have better prices, but there's no hard and fast rule in this regard. Luckily there are enough shops in the Old Town selling similar items that price comparison is easy.

Viru, Müürivahe and Lükike Streets

Viru is the Old Town's most commercial and touristy stretch. Nearby Müürivahe is worth exploring for its small, fashion boutiques. Anyone shopping for art, however, should head to Lühike Street, home of the **Lühikese Jala Galerii**. This is an excellent place to find ceramics, painted silk, etched glass, jewellery and other applied art. The shop is also interesting for the small spring, visible through a hole in the back room.

Paintings are sold up the hill at **Galerii 36**, Lühike 8. Across the street, at No. 5, is **Helina Tilk**, which sells kitchen ceramics, textiles and other home decor all featuring the artist's cats, dogs and barnyard animals.

Pikk Street

Head to the top of Lühike and through the gate tower towards Pikk, to find the shop belonging to another famous local artist, Navitrolla. His animal creations are sold at the **Navitrolla Galerii**, Pikk 7. At Pikk 9 is **Bogapott**, a combination of a pottery workshop, craft shop and café.

The more expensive of the Old Town's antiques shops tend to be bright and orderly, but the more fun ones are junk-shop affairs including Antikvaar (Rataskaevu 20) and Reval Antiik (Pikk 31). Pick up antique books at Raamatukoi (Viru 21 and Voorimehe 9).

Fashions and Household Goods

Less tourist-orientated shopping (fashion, housewares, etc) is concentrated in the downtown area, particularly in the large Viru Keskus shopping centre, just outside the Old Town, at Viru väljak 4–6. Look for Baltman and Monton shops here, which sell high-quality, locally produced clothing. The same mall houses the Kaubamaja department store, Estonia's largest. Stockmann, the Finnish department store, is a short walk down Rävala puiestee from here. Find it at Liivalaia 53.

Bargain hunters can find good deals in the nearby passenger port area at shopping centres that cater to discerningly frugal Finns. The newest is the Sadamarket, Sadama 6–8, an excellent place for bulk cigarette and alcohol purchases. The more market-like Merekeskus, Mere pst. 10, has stalls that sell everything from Estonian jumpers to suspiciously cheap CDs.

Markets

Those shopping for knits and other handicrafts should head straight to the markets. The most famous of these is the **knit market**, along the town wall on Müürivahe, opposite McDonald's. Here old ladies sell piles of hand-made knits of all descriptions.

During the summer tourist season, other Old Town **craft markets** operate in the Börsi passage, between Pikk 15 and 17, and in a small lot beside the Mere Puiestee tram stop. Arts and crafts markets also pop up periodically on and around Town Hall Square throughout the warmer months, and Tallinn's **Christmas Market** operates on the square from late November.

Market shoppers should beware that locals almost never haggle – the price they name is what they expect to get.

Crafts and Antiques

Another destination for intriguing craft shopping is **St Catherine's Guild** in Katariina käik (St Catherine's Passage), a row of open workshops where you can watch artists create blown-glass wares, ceramics, quilts, hats and other items.

The most authentic craft shops in Tallinn are those run by the **Eesti Käsitöö** organisation. They have branches in large malls, but in the Old Town they're at Raekoja plats 17, Kuninga 1 and Pikk 22.

Anyone looking specifically for wooden souvenirs should check out the Puupood, Lai 5. Doll collectors, likewise, should head to the Nukupood, Raekoja plats 18.

Above and right: craftwork at St Catherine's Guild

EATING OUT

When Estonians want to spice up a dish, they use salt. When they're feeling really wild, they add a dash of pepper…or so the local saying goes. There's just no getting around it – Estonian food is, in a word, bland, and some traditional dishes are definitely not for the squeamish. Still, there's enough variety on Estonian menus that you're bound to find something you like.

What is now termed 'traditional Estonian cuisine' developed from a base of centuries-old Estonian village culture, with a large dash of German, Slavic and Scandinavian influence thrown in. It can be found in grandmothers' kitchens throughout the countryside, as well as in a few Tallinn restaurants that cater specifically to tourists. Classics include *sült*, jellied pork typically served cold with a spot of mustard; *marineeritud angejras* (marinated eel); *mulgikapsad* (sauerkraut stew with pork); Baltic sprats; and *keel* (tongue). Various types of *vorst* (sausage) also appear, the most cherished being *verivorst* (blood sausage), which is served during the Christmas season.

Another winter favourite is *hernesupp*, pea soup made with bacon or pork. *Kama*, a cold, part-liquid type substance made from ground grains and peas, is the quintessential, old-fashioned dessert.

It's important to make a distinction here between this 'traditional' category of cuisine, usually reserved for special occasions, and what Estonians actually eat when they rush out to lunch. Today's Estonian food, which you'll find in nearly every small café and pub, consists mostly of simple meat-and-potatoes dishes, with pork playing a major role. Nearly every menu will have some combination of *seakarbonaad* (pork chops), *paneeritud sealiha* (breaded pork), *grillitud sealiha* (grilled pork), *kanafilee* (chicken fillet), *grillitud forell* (grilled salmon) and other protein-heavy choices. These are typically served with fried, boiled or baked potatoes. If you can't make up your mind, or you're low on cash, you can always order the *päevapraad* (weekday lunch special), which will fill you up for about 30–40kr.

During Soviet times, a number of popular dishes drifted in from other parts of the USSR and now feature prominently on Estonian menus. These include *seljanka*, a salty, Russian meat soup; *pelmeenid*, pork dumplings usually served in broth; and the all-time summer favourite, *čačlõkk*, a grilled shish-kebab that originates from the Caucasus region.

Above: trendy lunch. **Right:** stylishly presented cuisine at the restaurant of the Three Sisters Hotel *(see pages 88–89)*

Another local menu nuance in Estonia is that *pannkoogid* (pancakes) and *omletid* (omelettes) are not just for breakfast. Both can be filled with savoury items such as ham and cheese, chicken or tuna, and are served at lunch and dinner. Pancakes filled with jam are also a common dessert.

If all of this sounds a bit too unfamiliar, you'll be happy to know that Tallinn is home to a sophisticated restaurant scene, where everything from fajitas to sushi is available. Ethnic and international restaurants abound, and in the Old Town they far outnumber those serving Estonian food. But even here you'll notice that some daring chefs have found ways of integrating exotic local ingredients into their menus – Tallinn may be the only city in the world where you can find moose curry (Elevant) and bear sausages (Olde Hansa).

Restaurants in Tallinn are typically open from noon to 11pm or midnight, closing a little later on Fridays and Saturdays. The price categories below are based on the approximate cost of a meal for one person, including a soup or salad, a main course, and a glass of wine or beer.

$ = 100–225kr
$$ = 225–350kr
$$$ = 350–600kr

Estonian

Eesti Maja
Lauteri 1
Tel: 6455 252
With the widest range of national dishes available – everything from marinated eel to pancakes – this city-centre cellar restaurant is the best choice for anyone who wants to experience the full spectrum of traditional favourites. Diners can opt for the casual, roomy main hall or one of the cosier rooms at the back. In either case, they'll find a relaxed, slightly folksy atmosphere. $$

Kulse Notsu Kõrts
Dunkri 8
Tel: 6286 567
Wooden benches, whitewashed walls and kitchen utensils hanging from the rafters create a romanticised, village look at the Golden Piggy Tavern. Its attachment to the Hotel St Petersburg gives it a definite tourist orientation, but prices are very reasonable and the menu includes lots of intriguing items like wild boar stew and 'Old Witch's mushroom-and-onion casserole'. $$

Vanaema Juures
Rataskaevu 10–12
Tel: 6269 080
By far Tallinn's cosiest cellar restaurant, Grandma's Place is brimming with old photos, antiques and grandmotherly charm. The consistently tasty food on offer is a mix of established, national dishes, Estonian game and the chef's own inventions. Because of the restaurant's small size and popularity, it's best to book in advance during the tourist season. Closes early on Sunday. $$

Medieval

Olde Hansa
Vana Turg 1
Tel: 6279 020
Despite being unabashedly touristy, Olde Hansa offers the one dining experience you won't want to miss on a visit to Tallinn. Wooden tables, candle lighting, live chamber music, chatty waiters in period costume and dozens of other details create an unforgettable, medieval atmosphere in this three-storey restaurant. The high-quality food ranges from almond chicken to bear. Reserve. $$

International

Admiral
Lootsi 15
Tel: 6623 777
This is a tiny, elegant restaurant, built into an old steamship docked at Tallinn's port. A mix of Slavic and Balkan meat dishes, as well as seafood, makes up the menu. Ask for a table on the side that faces town, for better views. **$$**

Café Zebra
Narva mnt. 7
Tel: 6109 230
With its slick, modern set-up, Café Zebra works both as a classy, order-at-the-counter lunch spot (sushi, salads and pastries are on display), and as a relaxed, à-la-carte restaurant, where casual gourmet fare is on offer. Count on top-notch homemade desserts and excellent service. **$$$**

Gloria
Müürivahe 2
Tel: 6446 950
The decadence of the late 1930s, when this restaurant was originally opened, comes through in every aspect of this high-class, gourmet establishment. A mixture of European and Russian classics is available, complemented by a choice of more than 700 different wines from across the world. **$$$**

Pegasus
Harju 1
Tel: 6314 040
Award-winning chefs and an ever-changing menu of inventive 'world cuisine' keep Pegasus at the top of the list of Tallinn's modern, upscale restaurants. The slick, multi-storeyed interior includes large windows that overlook Niguliste Church. The ground-floor bar is also known as one of the city's more sophisticated nightspots. **$$$**

Sisalik
Pikk 30
Tel: 6446 542
This small cellar restaurant is praised for its quality food and intimate atmosphere. The menu is a combination of Southern European and French food and includes tapas, pasta and creative appetisers. **$$**

Stefanie's
Maakri 19–21
Tel: 6612 612
The location near the Radisson Hotel means that Stefanie's is frequented by a suited business crowd at lunch, but the slick-yet-soft ambience lets it work well as a relaxed dinner destination. Light grilled items, soups and pastas make up the modern, European-style menu. **$$**

Seafood

Mõõkkala
Kuninga 4
Tel: 6418 288
Elegant, arty decor and a clever use of mood lighting give the Old Town's première fish restaurant, Mõõkkala (meaning 'swordfish'), an almost dreamy look. The real attraction, though, is the cuisine, with every kind of seafood from oysters to shark, expertly prepared. **$$**

ö

Mere pst. 6E
Tel: 5616 150

Though this trendy establishment near the port doesn't bill itself as a seafood restaurant fish dishes make up most of the menu. Catering to a young, professional set, it has a decidedly upmarket feel, but doesn't descend into stiff formality. **$$$**

Ethnic

African Kitchen
Uus 34
Tel. 6442 555

A combination of hip, vibrant decor and mouth-watering meals prepared by African chefs make this an excellent choice for a casual meal. DJs occasionally play reggae on weekends. **$**

Bocca
Olevimägi 9
Te : 6412 610

A very stylish, contemporary take on what an Italian restaurant should be, Bocca attracts its fair share of Tallinn's elite, as well as a few savvy foreigners. Among the more original items available is ravioli stuffed with rabbit in a tarragon, walnut and mushroom sauce. Reserve. **$$$**

Café VS
Pärnu mnt. 28
Tel: 6272 627

This trendy, chrome-filled bar is the place to go in Tallinn for an informal, Indian meal. Excellent curries, tikkas, biryanis and a fun, busy atmosphere. **$**

Controvento
Vene 12 (in Katariina käik)
Tel: 6440 470

For years this classic Italian restaurant has been a mainstay of Tallinn's fine dining scene, made all the more inviting by its location in a snug, medieval passageway. The long menu includes beef fillets, stuffed pasta and thin, Italian-style pizza. Reserve in summer and at weekends. **$$**

Elevant
Vene 5
Tel: 6313 132

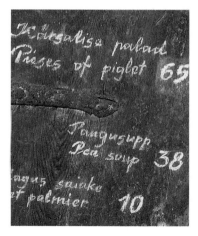

Climb the iron spiral staircase to enter this sophisticated Indian restaurant. Its relaxing, warm, tropical tones and wicker furniture encourage unrushed dining. **$$**

Golden Dragon
Pikk 37
Tel: 6313 506

Of the many Chinese restaurants in Tallinn, this busy cellar venue in the Old Town provides the tastiest food and best service. **$$**

Gianni
Jõe 4a
Tel: 6263 684

Slightly out of Old Town, this swanky Italian restaurant is nevertheless worth a visit for its excellent pasta and professional service. **$$**

Pizza Americana
Müürivahe 2
Tel: 6448 837

This fun, red-, white-and-blue café offers dozens of varieties of thick, hearty pizza, all served in an iron pan. Unless you have an inhumanly big stomach, order the small. **$**

Silk
Kullassepa 4
Tel: 6484 625

A huge range of sushi, not to mention other Japanese favourites, is served in this slick, black-lined café just off Town Hall Square. For something different, try the green tea ice-cream. **$$**

Left: *sült,* a traditional dish made of jellied pork
Above: dish of the day

Troika
Raekoja plats 15
Tel: 6276 245
Lavishly decorated with thick, red drapes and paintings of village life, this cellar restaurant represents the stylised extreme of Russian dining. All the classics from *blini* (pancakes) to stroganoff are available, and a Russian folk singer occasionally performs old standards. $$

Villa Thai
Vilmsi 6
Tel: 6419 347
Tasty Thai and Indian cuisine is cooked up in this soothingly decorated establishment in the Kadriorg district. It's worth the trip out here from the Old Town to dine among the elephants, Buddhas and bamboo. $$

Cafés & Cheap, Casual Eateries

Chocolaterie
Vene 6
Tel: 6418 061
Tucked away in an Old Town courtyard, this place is worth a visit for its hand-made truffles and cosy 19th-century atmosphere. $

Karja Kelder
Väike-Karja 1
Tel: 6441 008
Try this classic, Estonian cellar pub for a dose of local atmosphere and a taste of what the locals like to eat. Good beer selection. $

Kehrwieder
Saiakang 1
An arty, cave-like establishment, Kehrwieder provides a real escape from the outside world, even with one of its rooms opening onto Town Hall Square. Excellent coffee. $

Kompressor
Rataskaevu 3
Tel: 6464 210
Cheap, enormous pancakes filled with things such as garlic cheese, smoked turkey, shrimp and ham are the mainstays at this popular student hangout. $

Maiasmokk
Pikk 16
Tel: 6464 066
Dating to 1864, Maiasmokk (Sweet Tooth) is Tallinn's oldest café. It's often crammed with old ladies who come for the cheap coffee and cakes, but drop in anyway for a look at the elaborate, old-style interior. $

Moskva
Vabaduse väljak 10
Tel: 6404 694
Tallinn's beautiful and trendy set flocks to this slick, two-storey café for drinks and light meals. It's also a popular night spot, with the larger, upstairs section occasionally used as a disco lounge. $

Above: Viru Bar

NIGHTLIFE

In a city where the younger generation holds so much sway, it's not surprising that Tallinn's nightlife is defined by raucous, alcohol-fuelled partying. The Old Town, with its high concentration of bars and pubs, is the city's most active drinking and dancing zone. In fact, the area is so small that it's not unusual for friends to migrate from bar to bar all evening, finally settling in wherever they find the best music and crowd.

Friday night, and to a slightly lesser extent Saturday night, is when most Tallinners go out, filling up the pubs from about 10pm and moving on to the clubs between midnight and 1am. Other nights are relatively dead – most nightclubs don't even bother opening from Sunday to Tuesday. This pattern changes somewhat during summer, when tourists and holidaying students keep other evenings lively.

Local tastes have become more sophisticated over the last five years or so, and the variety of drinking establishments available has moved beyond the earthy beer bars and kitschy, Irish-style pubs that dominated here in the 1990s. Stylish, busy lounge bars, many with weekend DJs, are frequented by the city's movers and shakers.

Those looking for a quieter evening usually prefer the Old Town's intimate wine bars. With plush surroundings and soft music, they're by far the cosiest places to drink. Cigar lounges offer similar shelter for anyone who prefers relaxing with a Cohiba and a brandy.

Culture creatures should note that in Tallinn, classical concerts, opera and ballet usually start in the early evening, at 7pm. An updated list of Tallinn's daily cultural offerings can be obtained from the Tallinn Tourist Information Centre; Niguliste 2/ Kullassepa 4; tel: 6457 777. The same information is listed on www.tourism.tallinn.ee.

Tickets to classical events promoted by the nation's classical event organiser, Eesti Kontsert, are sold at the Estonia Concert Hall's ticket office, Estonia pst. 4; tel: 6147 760; open Mon–Fri noon–7pm, Sat noon–5pm, and one hour before the start of concerts. Tickets to other major events are sold at distributors such as Piletilevi at the Viru

shopping centre's information point, Viru väljak 4–6. and Piletimaailm, attached to the Tallinna Kaubamaja department store, Gonsiori 2. Note that theatre in Tallinn is conducted almost exclusively in Estonian and Russian. Cinema goers will be happy to know, however, that all films (except cartoons) are shown in their original language with Estonian subtitles.

Cinemas

Coca-Cola Plaza
Hobujaama 5
With 11 screens, this is Tallinn's largest and most modern cinema, and the best place to see the latest Hollywood blockbusters. The paid information line, tel: 1182, provides current listings in English.

Kosmos
Pärnu mnt. 45
After films leave the Coca-Cola Plaza they play at this two-screen cinema at a reduced price. The same information line, tel: 1182, has the schedules.

Sõprus
Vana-Posti 8
Tel: 6441 919
Art-house and other non-mainstream films.

Opera, Classical Music & Ballet

Estonia Concert Hall/
Estonian National Opera
Estonia pst. 4
Tel: 6147 760 (concerts), 6831 260 (opera, ballet)
Built in 1913, bombed in 1944, reconstructed in 1947 and then renovated in 2005, the grand old Estonia Concert Hall (popularly known as the 'Estonia Theatre') is Tallinn's all-in-one house of culture. One wing houses the main stage of Eesti Kontsert, the nation's classical concert organiser, while the other is used for operas and ballets that fall under the auspices of the Estonian National Opera.

Kanuti Gildi Saal
Pikk 20
Tel: 6464 704
The city's premiere venue for modern ballet performances.

favourites. Check their schedule, www.rock cafe.ee, before making the trip.

Von Krahli Baar
Rataskaevu 10–12
Tel: 6269 090
This quirky theatre bar is home to an arty, student crowd, and is the best place in Tallinn to hear up-and-coming bands.

Bars & Pubs
Café VS
Pärnu mnt. 28
Tel: 6272 627
Slick, modern, busy and fun, VS is a worthy destination for progressive DJ music, excellent Indian food or just a place to drink.

Hell Hunt
Pikk 39
Tel: 6818 333
The Gentle Wolf is the best place in Tallinn to grab a beer with friends. It has the rare quality of being both lively and local, and serves decent pub food.

Karja Kelder
Väike-Karja 1
Tel: 6441 008
For the most authentic Estonian pub experience, head to this tavern-style cellar bar and eat garlic bread with the locals. Live bands some weekends.

Nimega Baar
Suur-Karja 13
Tel: 6209 299
The popular 'Pub with a Name' is an integral part of the Old Town's drinking scene. DJs and dancing in the back.

Nimeta Baar
Suur-Karja 4
Tel: 6411 515
Just up the street from its counterpart, the 'Pub with no Name' is more of a sports bar, but also has weekend DJs and decent pub food.

St Patrick's
Suur-Karja 8
Tel: 6418 173
Despite the Irish name, St Patrick's has a local feel and an unusual, medieval interior.

Drama Theatres
Eesti Draamateater
Pärnu mnt. 5
Tel: 6805 555
Classics of the Estonian and world stage are performed in the two halls of this Art Nouveau theatre.

Tallinna Linnateater
Lai 23
Tel: 6650 800
The city's most famous troupe makes its home in this renovated Old Town building.

Vene Draamateater
Vabaduse väljak 5
Tel: 6418 246
Estonia's state Russian theatre.

Live Music
Guitar Safari
Müürivahe 22
Tel: 6411 607
A small, Old Town cellar venue mostly featuring unknown rock and blues bands.

Kolumbus Krisostomus
Viru 24
Tel: 5615 6924
One of Estonia's rock legends can usually be found playing this beer-hall-style venue above McDonald's.

Rock Café
Tartu mnt. 80d
Tel: 5695 8888
Though it's far from the centre, Rock Café nevertheless pulls in some of the nation's

Above: cultural sign
Right: bright lights at Hell Hunt

Lounge Bars

Kaheksa (Lounge 8)
Vane-Posti 8
Tel: 6274 770
A trendy and slightly tropical hangout that is frequented by a fashionable clientele. Serves excellent smoothies.

Pegasus
Harju 1
Tel: 6314 040
The ground floor of the Pegasus restaurant is home to a chic bar. It's especially popular when the summer terrace is open.

Popular
Vana-Viru 6
Tel: 6414 565
Chilled out twenty-somethings flock here to smoke water pipes.

Stereo Lounge
Harju 6
Tel: 6310 549
Made up of one large, all-white room, Stereo Lounge tends to be loud and lively once the DJ starts playing.

Wine Bars

Gloria Veinikelder
Müürivahe 2
Tel. 6448 846
The restaurant's elaborately decorated wine cellar offers unforgettable surroundings as well as Tallinn's largest choice of wines.

Kolme Näoga Mees
Kuninga 1
Tel: 6484 251
This romantic, Old Town cellar is deservedly a Tallinn favourite.

Musi
Niguliste 6
Tel: 6443 100
Set apart by its artistic interior, Musi is well worth a look.

Veinipööning
Viru 18
Tel: 6418 631
The Wine Attic is cleverly filled with antique furniture and even beds.

Cigar Rooms

Davidoff Sigari Maja
Raekoja plats 16
Tel: 6314 735
Oozes classic, old-fashioned elegance befitting the mid-20th-century aristocracy.

La Casa del Habano
Dunkri 2
Tel: 6445 647
Tallinn's exclusive Cuban cigar importer has a small, relaxed lounge.

Nightclubs

Angel
Sauna 1
Tel: 6416 880

Tallinn's largest gay disco is somewhat exclusive, but all are very welcome at the Angel Café upstairs.

BonBon
Mere pst. 6e
Tel: 6616 080
More urbane and expensive than its rivals, BonBon is the favourite of Tallinn's young, moneyed set.

Club Privé
Harju 6
Tel: 6310 545
A small yet sophisticated club above Stereo Lounge. Famous DJs are the major draw.

Hollywood
Vana-Posti 8
Tel: 6274 770
The Old Town's largest, most popular disco attracts droves of foreign men and local teenage blondes.

Terrarium
Sadama 6
Tel: 6614 721
A fairly standard, busy disco near the port.

Venus Club
Vana-Viru 14
Tel: 6418 184
Smaller and more local than Hollywood, Venus is known for its go-go dancers and weekend events.

CALENDAR OF EVENTS

Organisers pack nearly all of Tallinn's outdoor festivals into the June–August period, but there are also indoor events to keep the masses entertained through the long winter nights. The best source of information on current and upcoming events is the Tallinn Tourist Information Centre, tel: 6457 777, www.tourism.tallinn.ee.

Apart from music festivals, markets and other organised activities, Tallinn's calendar is dotted with a number of religious and folk holidays, some of which trace their roots to Estonia's pre-Christian agricultural traditions.

Vastlapäev (Shrove Tuesday), a floating holiday in February, is celebrated with sledding, pea soup and special pastries. On 30 April, **Wolbriöö** (Witch's Night) is an excuse for young people to dress up in costumes and drink to excess. The largest holiday of the year, barring Christmas, is **Jaanipäev** (St John's Day or Midsummer) on 24 June. Estonians celebrate it by heading to the countryside on the evening prior for a night of bonfires and beer. Cemeteries fill with candles on 2 November, **Hingedepäev** (All Souls' Day), the day to honour the dead.

As in other Protestant countries, Estonians celebrate **Christmas** on 25 December, with a special emphasis on Christmas Eve.

January–February

The **opeNBaroque** music festival, a two-week concert series held in late-January or

February, showcases European Baroque with a particular emphasis on Tallinn's own early music group, **Hortus Musicus**. Concerts take place in intriguing, Old Town locations, and musical styles from various world cultures are also included in the mix. For details, contact Eesti Kontsert, Estonia pst. 4, tel: 6147 700, www.concert.ee.

February also marks the annual return of **Student Jazz**, a youth jazz and rhythm festival. Check www.tudengijazz.ee for the current year's venue and dates.

March–April

Tallinn's modern dance organiser, the Kanuti Gildi Saal, tel: 6464 704, www.saal.ee, shows off the cutting-edge innovations in Estonia's active dance scene with **Uus Tants** (New Dance), a three-day event held at the end of March.

In late April, Estonia's major jazz festival, **Jazzkaar**, attracts a good number of first-class international guest performers. Apart from mainstream and avant-garde jazz, the programme also includes interesting selections of blues and world music. Concerts are held at various locations throughout the city. For performance times and ticket details, contact Jazzkaar, tel: 6114 405, www.jazzkaar.ee.

May–June

The international music festival, **Tubin and his Time**, is held in late-May or June to honour Estonia's most revered symphonist, Eduard Tubin (1905–82).

Tallinn turns medieval during **Old Town Days**, an event-packed festival at the beginning of June. For three days, performers in 14th-century costume bring time-honoured Tallinn traditions back to life with activities like an archery contest, jousting and medieval crafts making. At the same time, more modern entertainment, from brass bands to dance shows, fills every free space in the Old Town.

Estonia's all-important midsummer holiday, **Jaanipäev** (St John's Day), is not an urban event, but on the evening of 23 June visitors can join the traditional festivities held at the Estonian Open Air Museum, tel: 6549 100, www.evm.ee. *See also Itinerary* ⸮ *pages 54–57.*

July–August

The first week of July brings the city's massive beer bash, **Beer Summer**, the most popular festival of the year. Held in the Song Festival Grounds, the five-day, family-style event involves a full schedule of live rock and jazz music, amusement park rides, games and activities for children, food tents and dozens of sorts of beer. For details, contact Meediaekspress, tel: 6112 112, www.ollesummer.ee.

At roughly the same time, the Estonian Folk Art Union runs a **Medieval Market** in which costumed merchants sell their wares in Town Hall Square and the nearby streets.

Tallinn's international contemporary dance festival, **August Tants**, takes place for two weeks in August. Contact the Kanuti Gildi Saal, tel: 6464 704, www.saal.ee.

Late-August also marks the time of the **Birgitta Festival**, a week of outdoor concerts presented by the Tallinn Philharmonic Society, set in the stunning ruins of St Bridget's Convent.

September

Tallinn's churches fill with song for one week in September as the **Credo International Festival of Sacred Music**, a concert series dedicated to the Virgin Mary, highlights Orthodox music both ancient and modern.

November–December

The long, winter nights of late November and early December become brighter with the coming of the highly popular **Black Nights Film Festival**, tel: 6284 510, www.poff.ee. World cinema, with an emphasis on European films, is the main focus, though Black Nights also includes sub-festivals showing student films, animation and children's films.

Late November also sees the arrival of Town Hall Square's annual **Christmas Market**, which typically lasts until December 25th. Bright lights, snow-covered market huts and music give the area a magical quality, and the Jõuluvana (Santa) makes his occasional cameo appearance.

The season is also marked by **Christmas Jazz**, a series of performances in theatres and churches around town. Contact Jazzkaar for details, tel: 6114 405, www.jazzkaar.ee.

Left: Song and Dance Festival

Practical
Information

GETTING THERE

By Air

Direct flights connect Tallinn Airport (tel: 6058 888, www.tallinn-airport.ee) to over 20 European cities, and, thanks to increased competition, prices have dropped dramatically in recent years. Estonian Air (www.estonian-air.com) offers competitive fares, particularly when booked online. EasyJet (www.easyjet.com) offers daily flights from London and Berlin. No long-haul flights land in Tallinn, but budget travellers from North America can look for deals to major European hubs such as London or Copenhagen, then continue on a cheap flight from there.

Tallinn Airport is tiny but modern and just 4km (2½ miles) from the city centre. City bus No. 2 leaves every 20 to 30 minutes from in front of the arrivals hall, making the 13-minute trip to the A. Laikmaa stop in the city centre. Tickets can be bought at the R-Kiosk in the arrivals hall for 10kr, or from the driver for 15kr. A taxi ride to the centre should cost about 70–90kr.

Travellers coming from Helsinki can also consider the fun but more expensive helicopter service run by Copterline (tel: 6101 818, www. copterline.ee), which makes the 85-km (52-mile) hop over the gulf in 18 minutes. Flights land at the Linnhall speedboat harbour, adjacent to the Old Town. Taxis to other parts of the centre cost about 50kr.

Airlines with offices in Tallinn include:
• **Czech Airlines**, Rävala pst. 5, tel: 6309 397, www.czechairlines.com
• **Estonian Air**, Vabaduse väljak 10, tel: 6401 163, www.estonian-air.com
• **Finnair**, Roosikrantsi 2, tel: 6110 950, www.finnair.com
• **LOT Polish Airways**, Tallinn Airport, tel: 6058 553, www.lot.com
• **Lufthansa**, Rävala pst. 6, tel: 6814 633, www.lufthansa.ee
• **SAS**, Tallinn Airport, tel: 6663 030, www.scandinavian.net

Left: St Olav's reflected in a car door
Right: sign to the Dominican Monastery

By Rail

Very few visitors get to Tallinn this way – the only international rail link is the daily train from Moscow. The overnight journey takes 15 hours and involves a gruelling, early-morning stop on the border for intensive passport and customs checks.

Tallinn's remodelled train station, the *Balti Jaam*, offers services including a luggage room, decent pay toilets and currency exchange. The Old Town is just a short hop from here, reachable via the grubby underground pedestrian passage to the left as you exit the main doors. Tram Nos 1 and 2 leave from behind the station, taking you to the city centre (on the other side of the Old Town) in four to five stops. Tickets cost 10kr from a kiosk in the station, or 15kr from the driver. A taxi to a hotel in the centre should cost no more than 50kr.

By Road

Coaches provide the cheapest and most convenient way to reach Tallinn from nearby Baltic cities. The trip from Riga takes just 5½ hours and costs about €12. From Vilnius it takes 10–11 hours to reach Tallinn; from St Petersburg 8–9 hours. Eurolines (tel: 6800 909, www.eurolines. com) and Ecolines (tel: 6101 570, www.ecolines.ee) handle international routes. Their coaches arriving from the south (Pärnu, Riga, Vilnius) make helpful stops in the city centre before reaching Tallinn's rather out-of-the-way bus station.

Once at Tallinn's coach station *(Bussijaam)*, you can take buses 17, 17A, 23 or 23A from the stop at the front of the station. From here it is just four stops to Vabaduse väljak, in the centre. Tram Nos 2 and 4 leave from Tartu mnt, across the large junction you'll face as you leave the station from its main doors.

These also reach the centre in four stops. A taxi ride to the centre should be about 50kr.

Drivers arriving from Latvia will find the border crossing fairly straightforward, with very short queues. In addition to your travel documents, you will usually be asked to show your vehicle registration and an internationally valid insurance policy. Taking cars to Estonia on the ferries from Finland is also quite common, and the same rules apply.

By Sea

Tallinn's Passenger Port *(Reisisadam)* is the main point of arrival for over two million travellers who visit from Finland and Sweden each year. Dozens of hydrofoils and catamarans make the 1½-hour crossing from Helsinki each day during the warmer months. In winter, ice and wind put a stop to the fast ship services, relegating traffic to the slower ferries, which take 3½–4 hours to cross the gulf. Tickets from Helsinki generally range from €14–30. There are also daily overnight ferries from Stockholm run by Tallink (tel: 6409 808, www.tallink.ee), and in summer, Silja Line (tel: 6116 661, www.silja.ee) operate an overnight service that leaves from St Petersburg and Rostock, Germany, every fourth day.

From the Passenger Port, the Old Town and centre are only a 10-minute walk. It might take about twice that long from the port's D-Terminal, where most large ferries arrive. In both cases, bus No. 2 will take you slightly further to the centre, but runs infrequently. A taxi ride to a central hotel should cost no more than 50–60kr.

Note that hydrofoils operated by Lindaline (tel: 6999 333, www.lindaliini.ee) arrive at the separate Linnahall harbour, located at the far end of a sprawling concrete structure northeast of the Passenger Port. Again, this is within easy walking distance of the centre and a taxi should be around 50kr.

Tallink and Silja, mentioned above, are major providers of ferry services from Helsinki. Other companies that operate ferries from Helsinki include:
• **Eckerö Line**, tel: 6318 606, www.eckeroline.ee
• **Nordic Jet Line**, tel: 6317 000, www.njl.info
• **Sea Wind Line**, tel: 6116 699, www.seawind.fi

TRAVEL ESSENTIALS

When to Visit

The bulk of visitors choose to come during the May–September period, when the weather is most bearable, the days are bright and long, and the Old Town atmosphere is at its liveliest. That said, a winter visit has its own rewards – nothing compares with the magical quality the Old Town has when covered by a fresh blanket of snow. A visit to the Christmas Market (open late-November to Christmas) is essential, made all the merrier by a steaming cup of *Hõõgwein* (spiced wine).

Visas and Passports

Citizens of the EU, EEA, US, Canada, Australia, New Zealand, Israel, Argentina, Japan and a number of other Asian and Latin American countries can enter Estonia and stay for up to 90 days without a visa. See the Estonian Foreign Ministry's website, www.vm.ee, for the complete list of nationals who can enter visa-free. Citizens of other countries, including Russia and the rest of the CIS, should contact their nearest Estonian consulate for a visa. South Africans do not need an Estonian visa if they hold a valid visa for Latvia or Lithuania. EU nationals can enter Estonia using national ID cards as travel documents. All others must have valid passports.

Vaccinations

No special vaccinations are required.

Customs

Since Estonia joined the EU in 2004, customs checks for those arriving from other member states have become practically non-existent, and limits on how much alcohol and tobacco you can bring in duty free are so high that they're not worth listing. Note, however, that Finland, Sweden and the UK restrict the number of cigarettes you can take back. If you're arriving from outside the EU, the international standard of 200 cigarettes, 1 litre of strong alcohol or two bottles of wine applies.

Weather

Summer is mostly mild and dry, although it can also range from clammy and drizzling to oppressively humid with thundery downpours. Estonia's northern latitude means the sum-

Right: walking towards the Russalka Memorial

mer sun rises at 4.30am and lingers until nearly midnight. Spring and autumn are typically chilly and damp. Winter is cold and dark, with the late-December sun setting just after 3pm.

Clothing

Standard, lightweight clothing is fine for summer, but a rainproof jacket, light jumper for chilly nights and good walking shoes are essential. Heavy winter gear is usually needed from November to March. Smart-casual dress is the most formal you'll need, even for upscale restaurants or the opera.

Electricity

Estonia uses standard continental European plugs. The current is 220 volts, 50Hz. Take an adaptor as necessary.

Time Differences

Throughout the year, Tallinn is two hours ahead of London, on a par with Helsinki and seven hours ahead of New York.

GETTING ACQUAINTED

Geography

Tallinn sits on the southern shore of the Gulf of Finland, on Estonia's north coast. The city is butterfly-shaped, pinched between the curve of Tallinn Bay at its northern edge and Lake Ülemiste in the south. With the exception of Toompea, Tallinn is mostly flat.

Government and Economy

Estonia is a parliamentary democracy. Members of its 101-seat *Riigikogu* (parliament) are chosen by general election every four years, and the *Riigikogu's* majority party or coalition in turn forms the nation's government. The Prime Minister holds the highest executive power, whereas the President, who is also chosen by the *Riigikogu*, serves in a mainly ceremonial capacity as head-of-state.

In recent years, both national and local politics have been a battle between the left-centrist Centre Party and a shaky coalition of three more conservative parties: Res Publica, Reform and People's Union. Far-reaching economic reforms introduced in the early 1990s have made Estonia's dynamic economy the envy of its Eastern European neighbours. Dubbed the 'Baltic Tiger', the country has enjoyed a steady, 6 percent GDP growth since 1995, and was ranked the 4th freest economy in the world by a *Wall Street Journal*/Heritage Foundation survey in 2005.

Religion

Despite the abundance of churches in Tallinn's Old Town, Estonia is fairly secular, with only 29 percent of its inhabitants claiming to follow any specific religious faith. Of those, 46 percent belong to the Lutheran Church, Estonia's traditional religion since the Reformation in the 16th century. Another 44 percent are Russian Orthodox. Baptists, Catholics and Jehovah's Witnesses make a small showing.

Population

Tallinn is by far Estonia's largest city, home to 400,000 of the nation's 1.35 million inhabitants. Most (54 percent) Tallinners are ethnic Estonian, descendants of Finno-Ugric tribes that moved into the northern Baltic region in the third millennium BC. Some 42 percent of Tallinners are 'Russian speakers', a local term that usually denotes ethnic Russians, but could also include Ukrainians and Belorussians. Though Russians have had a presence in Tallinn for centuries, most of today's 'Russian speakers' come from families sent to work in Estonia during the Soviet period.

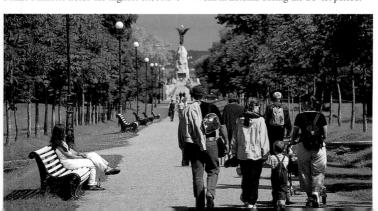

MONEY MATTERS

Currency

Estonia's currency is the *kroon*, abbreviated 'kr' or 'EEK'. It is pegged to the euro at €1 = 15.65kr. The *kroon* is divided into 100 *senti*. Bank notes come in denominations of 2, 5, 10, 25, 50, 100 and 500kr. The largest-value coin in common circulation is the 1kr. *Senti* coins (10s, 20s, 50s) are hardly used outside food shops and pharmacies.

Credit Cards

The Estonians' love affair with plastic means that all but the smallest shops and cafés take Visa and MasterCard. American Express, on the other hand, has yet to catch on, and is only accepted by major hotels and a few restaurants. Some taxis, such as those run by Tulika (tel: 1200) and Linnatakso (tel: 1242), accept credit cards, but check this when booking.

Cash advances on Visa and MasterCard cards are available at most banks. In the Old Town, you can use Hansapank (Viru 4) or SEB Eesti ühispank (Suur-Karja 20); both cash Amex and Visa travellers' cheques, but only ühispank accept Thomas Cook. American Express services are handled by the Estravel agency at Suur-Karja 15 (tel: 6266 266; open Mon–Fri 9am–6pm, Sat 10am–3pm).

Cash Machines

Cash machines are easy to find in Tallinn, and all accept international cards. The most central is at the Sampo Pank on Town Hall Square, Raekoja plats 8, and there's another nearby at Viru 4. Elsewhere in the Old Town they can be found at Viru 27A, Suur-Karja 18, Suur-Karja 20, Pikk 36, Aia 5, Harju 13 and Vabaduse Väljak 10.

Tipping

Though many locals have yet to adopt the habit, it has become customary to tip about 10 percent at sit-down restaurants. Tips aren't expected at cafés, pubs or anywhere you order and pay at the till, nor is it necessary to tip taxi drivers. Hotel porters expect about 20kr.

Taxes

Estonia's value-added tax (VAT) is 18 percent. All prices listed in restaurants, hotels, shops, etc include this tax.

Bureaux de Change

Banks such as Hansapank, SEB Eesti ühispank and Sampo (mentioned left) are the most common places to exchange money as they offer favourable rates on most currencies. Unfortunately, most are closed on weekends. A good alternative is the Tavid exchange (Aia 5; open Mon–Fri 9am–7pm, Sat 9am–5pm, Sun 10am–5pm), which often gives even better rates than banks on sums over 1,300kr or €200. Small exchange offices around the Old Town, particularly the tourist-oriented Monex offices, offer far worse deals and should be avoided.

GETTING AROUND

Taxis

All taxis in Tallinn run on meters and have rates posted on their doors, but somehow this doesn't stop a fair number of them from overcharging. Be especially wary of taxis waiting at the port, railway station or on the edges of the Old Town. You can avoid surprises by asking the driver for an estimate before you get in. The best way to prevent hassle is to order by phone. Tulika (tel: 1200), Linnatakso (tel: 1242, 6442 442) and the cheaper Silver (tel: 15 222, 6278 850) have proven reliable. Average fares include a base of 10–35kr, then 7kr per kilometre.

Buses, Trolleybuses and Trams

Tallinn has a fairly efficient public transport system serviced by buses, trolleybuses and trams, all of which use the same tickets. Trams are best for getting around the centre – they stop frequently, and there are only four lines (numbered 1–4) to negotiate. Buses will take you to attractions out of the centre.

Several tickets are available. A single-ride ticket *(talong)* costs 10kr from a kiosk (a book of ten is 80kr), or 15kr from the driver. Once on board, slide this ticket into the green-topped, mechanical punch and pull it forward to validate it. Other tickets are time-sensitive passes sold in kiosks. They include a 1-hour (15kr), 2-hour (18kr), 24-hour (40kr) and 72-hour (80kr) ticket. Validate these on your first ride by placing them in the electronic punch inside the vehicle, which marks the time and date. Vehicles don't have conductors, but

Right: in summer bicycle taxis *(velotaksod)* become part of the Old Town landscape

inspectors do randomly board to check tickets. If you're caught without one, you'll be charged a 600kr fine, payable on the spot.

Coach

Cheap, frequent connections have made coach travel the most popular method of getting around Estonia and the Baltics. Tallinn's coach station *(Bussijaam)* at Lastekodu 46 can be reached by trams 2 or 4 from the centre. Tickets to domestic locations are sold in the main hall, but can also be bought from the driver. The www.bussiresid.ee website lists schedules in English.

International routes are handled by Eurolines and Ecolines. The Eurolines office (tel: 6800 909, www.eurolines.com) is located in the coach terminal, upstairs. Ecolines (tel: 6101 570, www.ecolines.ee) has its office in the downtown Viru Centre.

Train

Compared to coaches, trains are a much less practicable way to get around Estonia, but it is possible to reach larger cities by rail. Note that the only international route is the daily train to Moscow.

Tallinn's train station is the *Balti Jaam* (Toompuiestee 37, tel: 1447). Timetables are confusing, but at the information booth there's usually an English speaker who can help. Tickets to larger towns within Estonia are sold at window 3, international tickets at windows 4–6. In the same hall, an automated ticket machine with a touch screen will give you the schedules in English.

Car

If you just want to see Tallinn, a car will be more of a headache than a help, but if you're planning to tour the Estonian countryside or take the Lahemaa National Park excursion listed in this guide, car hire is sensible.

International firms such as **Avis** (tel: 6671 500, www.avis.ee), **Budget** (tel: 6058 600, www.budget.ee) and **Hertz** (tel: 6058 923, www.hertz.ee) have desks at Tallinn Airport. Local equivalents, including **R-Rent** (tel: 6058 929, www.rrent.ee) and **Sixt** (tel: 6058 148, www.sixt.ee), offer comparable service at a lower price.

Drivers should beware that most of the Old Town is a pedestrian zone, and finding free parking in central Tallinn is next to impossible. The simplest solution is to use a car park such as the one on Vabaduse väljak at the edge of the Old Town – or the city-centre parking garages at Rävala 5 and at the corner of Rävala and Maakri.

Ferry

Fast ferries provide an easy way to get to Helsinki, making the trip in just 1½ hours in summer. Ships leave from the Passenger Port *(Reisisadam)* at the end of Sadama street just outside the Old Town, and from the nearby Linnahall speedboat harbour. *See page 84* for details on ferry companies.

HOURS & HOLIDAYS

Business Hours

Offices are typically open weekdays, 9am–5pm. Smaller shops generally open at 10am and keep their doors open until 6 or 7pm on weekdays; most close at 3 or 4pm on Saturdays and stay closed on Sundays. Malls and department stores usually stay open from 9am to 9 or 10pm, even at weekends.

Public Holidays

1 January – New Year's Day
24 February – Independence Day
March/April (variable) – Good Friday
March/April (variable) – Easter Sunday
1 May – Spring Day
23 June – Victory Day
24 June – Midsummer's Day
20 August – Restoration of Independence
24 December – Christmas Eve
25 December – Christmas Day
26 December – Boxing Day

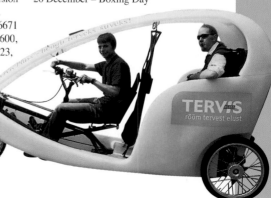

ACCOMMODATION

Tallinn's current tourism boom has led to a huge amount of investment money being poured into the hotel industry over the last few years. High-end accommodation is mostly divided between cosy, boutique-style hotels in the Old Town, and larger, modern establishments in the city centre that offer conference rooms, nightclubs and other such amenities. Hotels on the city's outskirts have traditionally filled the budget niche, but affordable, tourist-class hotels have now started appearing in and around the Old Town as well.

Nearly all hotels, with the exception of one or two of the budget establishments, offer direct-dial phones and satellite TV. Most also provide high-speed internet connections, either LAN or wireless. Price categories here are based on the cost of a standard double or twin room during high season (May–September).

$ = 500–1,000kr
$$ = 1,000–2,000kr
$$$ = 2,000–3,000kr
$$$$ = 3,000–6,000kr

Expensive

Hotel Barons
Suur-Karja 7/Väike Karja 2
Tel: 6999 700, fax: 6999 710
www.baronshotel.ee

Originally built as a commercial bank in 1912, this striking, Art Nouveau structure now houses one of Tallinn's most elegant hotels. A strong sense of early 20th-century chic runs throughout, from the sweeping staircase and caged lift in the lobby to guest rooms with high ceilings and antique-style furniture. The Old Town location and views from the restaurant are bonuses. $$$

Merchant's House Hotel
Dunkri 4–6
Tel: 6977 500, fax: 6977 501
www.merchantshousehotel.com
This 37-room boutique-style hotel makes its home in a pair of historic houses just off Town Hall Square. In addition to wooden-beamed ceilings and mysteriously twisting corridors, it offers a respectable café, restaurant and 'Ice Bar'. Rooms themselves are done in a modern, tasteful style. $$$$

Radisson SAS
Rävala 3
Tel: 6823 000, fax: 6823 001
www.radissonsas.com
The world-renowned chain is represented in Tallinn by a gleaming 24-storey glass high-rise in the city centre. Facilities include two restaurants, multiple conference rooms, a fully equipped gym and a sauna. Rooms come in Scandinavian, Italian, Oriental and maritime motifs, but the best are those with views towards the Old Town nearby. $$$

St Petersbourg Hotel
Rataskaevu 7
Tel: 6286 500, fax: 6286 565
www.schlossle-hotels.com
The same outfit that runs the acclaimed Schlössle *(right)* has given Tallinn's oldest hotel a similar level of hominess and old-fashioned charm, as well as an upscale Russian restaurant and folksy Estonian restaurant. Some guest rooms are on the small side. $$$$

Scandic Palace
Vabaduse väljak 3
Tel: 6407 300, fax: 6407 299
www.scandic-hotels.com
Though not the magnet for VIPs it was in the 1990s, the Palace is still appreciated for delivering 1930s-style elegance in a con-

Left: room at the exquisite Three Sisters

venient location next to the Old Town. The lobby restaurant and bar here are favourite meeting places for savvy locals. $$$

Schlössle Hotel

Pühavaimu 13–15
Tel: 6997 700, fax: 6997 777
www.schlossle-hotels.com
An elaborate, medieval-themed interior and award-winning restaurant were probably what helped Schlössle become Tallinn's first five-star hotel, but lots of nice in-room extras such as brass taps and bath-robes keep it at the top of the list. With just 24 rooms, it has a cosy, exclusive feel. $$$$

The Three Sisters

Pikk 71
Tel: 6306 300, fax: 6306 301
www.threesistershotel.com
The newer of Tallinn's two five-star hotels is built into the Three Sisters medieval dwelling houses on the quiet end of the Old Town's longest street. The interior is a tasteful mix of historic touches, including candle-lighting and canopy beds, and modern conveniences such as in-room DVD players. Some rooms even have a piano. $$$$

Moderate

Baltic Hotel Imperial

Nunne 14
Tel: 6274 800, fax: 6274 801
www.imperial.ee
This 38-room hotel at the edge of the Old Town has a distinctly historic feel, partly thanks to a section of the medieval town wall that runs through it. Downstairs are a decent pub and a cheese-themed restaurant. $$$

Baltic Hotel Vana Wiru

Viru 11
Tel: 6691 500, fax: 6691 501
www.vanawiru.ee
A very respectable, tourist-class hotel in a great Old Town location. Apart from a beautiful lobby, facilities include a conference room, two saunas, an Italian restaurant and a pub. $$

Domina Inn City

Vana-Posti 11–13
Tel: 6813 900, fax: 6813 901
www.dominahotels.ee

Marble-and-palm elegance in the heart of the Old Town's busiest pub and club area. All rooms come with internet-connected computers. $$$

Meriton Grand Hotel Tallinn

Toompuiestee 27
Tel: 6677 000, fax: 6677 555
www.meritonhotels.com
Located just outside the Old Town but away from the commercial centre, this modern, full-service facility offers everything from a beauty salon to an excellent bakery café. Some rooms have excellent views of the castle. $$$

Olevi Residents

Olevimägi 4
Tel: 6277 650, fax: 6277 651
www.olevi.ee
A cosy establishment with old-fashioned decor in a curious Old Town house. $$

Reval Hotel Olümpia

Liivalaia 33
Tel: 6315 333, fax: 6315 325
www.revalhotels.com
This enormous, central high-rise was built for the 1980 Olympics, but renovations in 2003 have made it world-class. Facilities include a large conference centre, popular nightclub and a 26th-floor health club/swimming pool with spectacular views. $$$

Scandic St Barbara

Roosikrantsi 2a
Tel: 6407 600, fax 6407430
www.scandic-hotels.com
A respectable, well-run hotel adjacent to the Old Town. The few facilities include a lobby computer station and German restaurant. $$

Sokos Viru Hotel

Viru väljak 4
Tel: 6809 300, fax: 6809 236
www.viru.ee
With over 500 rooms, the Viru is Tallinn's biggest and busiest hotel, and is especially popular with Finnish tour groups. Advantages here are the convenient, central location, and the hotel's attachment to the city centre's largest shopping centre. Free entrance to the Café Amigo nightclub downstairs. $$$

Uniquestay
Paldiski mnt. 1
Tel: 6600 700, fax: 6616 176
www.uniquestay.com
This British-owned venture aims at providing something different with its cool, modern styling and trendy café. More expensive 'Zen' rooms have whirlpool baths and NASA-designed gravity-free chairs. **$$**

Budget
City Guesthouse
Pärnu mnt. 10
Tel: 6282 236, fax: 6282 237
www.cityguesthouse.ee
A good option for convenience over luxury, this Old Town guesthouse offers minimalist singles, doubles and dormitory rooms. Showers and toilets are in the corridor. **$**

City Hotel Portus
Uus-Sadama 23
Tel: 6806 600, fax: 6806 601
www.tallinnhotels.ee
This modern, 107-room place makes its mark by offering cheerful, well-equipped modern rooms, all at low prices. It's good for frugal travellers coming in by ship, due to its location by the Passenger Port's D-terminal. **$$**

Dzingel
Männiku tee 89
Tel: 6105 201, fax: 6105 245
www.dzingel.ee

Meriton Old Town Hotel
Lai 49
Tel: 6141 300, fax: 6141 311
www.meritonhotels.com
The priority is to provide tourist-class affordability in an Old Town location, though this 41-room hotel still offers a fair amount of historic charm and a nice café. Small rooms. **$$**

Reval ExpressHotel
Sadama 1
Tel: 6678 700, fax: 6678 800
www.revalhotels.com
Located next to the Passenger Port, the modern ExpressHotel is especially popular with Finnish shoppers. Services are minimal, but the restaurant is revered for its soup buffet. **$$**

Hotel Schnelli
Toompuiestee 37
Tel: 6310 100, fax: 6310 101
www.gohotels.ee
Built as part of the train station's 2005 renovation, Schnelli offers well-equipped rooms for budget travellers. The location adjacent to the Old Town means that some rooms have views of Toompea Hill. Cheaper ones face the railway tracks. **$–$$**

Hotel Skåne
Kopli 2C
Tel: 6678 300, fax: 6678 301
www.nordichotels.ee
An early-20th-century wooden building just behind the train station houses this 38-room hotel. Renovations have restored its historic feel, though its colourful café is modern. **$**

Other Accommodation
Academic Hostel
Akadeemia Tee 11
Tel: 6202 275, fax: 6202 276
www.academichostel.com
Although it is located 5km (3 miles) from the centre, this hostel attached to the Technical University has excellent facilities. The 108 rooms are all twins. **$**

Vana Tom
Väike-Karja 1
Tel: 6313 252, fax: 6120 511
www.hostel.ee
Dormitory bedrooms and double rooms in

Left: 'Zen' room at the Uniquestay

Tallinn's oldest hostel. Pluses are the prime Old Town location and the guest kitchen. $

Kalev SPA Hotel & Water Park
Aia 18
Tel: 6493 300, fax: 6493 301
www.kalevspa.ee
Families in particular will appreciate this new hotel that offers an indoor water park as well as full spa treatment packages. Convenient Old Town location. $$

Serviced Apartments

Rental apartments, most with modern renovation and central locations, can be economical, particularly for anyone staying for a week or longer. Reputable firms include:
• **Erel International**, Tartu mnt. 14, tel: 6108 780, fax: 6108 790, www.erel.ee
• **Ites Apartments**, Harju 6, tel: 6310 637 www.ites.ee

Campsites

• **Tallinn City Camping**, Pirita tee 28, tel: 6052 044, fax: 6137 429, www.tallinn-city-camping.ee
• **Pirita Harbour Camping**, Regati pst. 1, tel: 6398 980, www.piritatop.ee

HEALTH & EMERGENCIES

Hygiene/General Health

Visiting Estonia poses no significant health risks. Tallinn's tap water is perfectly safe to drink, though many locals prefer the taste of the bottled variety.

Pharmacies

Tallinn's pharmacies *(Apteek)* are fully stocked with familiar medicines, and pharmacists usually speak some English. The city's all-night pharmacy is the Tõnismäe Apteek (Tõnismägi 5, tel: 6442 282). Beware that Estonian pharmacies cannot fill prescriptions by foreign doctors.

Medical/Dental Services

Service at state-run hospitals can be haphazard, so most foreigners avoid them when they can. Private clinics are up to Western standards, but few provide emergency care. If you find yourself in need of medical attention, call the first-aid hotline run by Tallinn's paramedics (tel: 6971 145), who will give you advice and direct you to a hospital if needed. The dental clinic in the Olümpia Hotel (Liivalaia 33. tel: 6315 443, 5177 456) is the best to call for weekend/late-night dental emergencies. If you need an ambulance, call 112.

Crime/Police

Tallinn is a relatively quiet city, but foreign visitors do occasionally fall victim to street crime. Beware of pickpockets in the Old Town, particularly along Viru street. Avoid the train station, parks and unlit areas at night. To report a crime, contact the Central Police Station, at Pärnu mnt. 11, tel: 6124 200. Call 110 for police emergencies.

Toilets

Meeste (M) or a triangle pointing downwards signifies the gents' toilets; *naiste* (N) or a triangle pointing upwards indicates the ladies. Tallinn has few public toilets, but they're strategically located. There's one on Town Hall Square, hidden in the foyer of the Troika restaurant, Raekoja plats 15. On Toompea Hill, look for the free-standing, coin-operated booth next to Aleksander Nevsky Cathedral.

MEDIA & COMMUNICATIONS

Post

You can buy stamps and postcards from most newspaper kiosks, then drop your mail into one of the orange-and-blue Eesti Post boxes around town. For all other postal matters, head to Tallinn Post Office at Narva 1. It's open Mon–Fri 7.30am–8pm, Sat 9am–6pm and Sun 9am–3pm. The large hall upstairs handles most services, but packages are sent from a small office to the left side of the building.

Telephones

Estonia's country code is 372. Within Estonia, you don't need codes to call other cities or regions. For domestic calls, including those to mobile phones, just dial the number as listed. Public phones in Tallinn operate with phone cards, sold at newspaper kiosks in denominations of 30, 50 and 100kr. These phones can be used for international calls.

For calls abroad, dial the international access code, 00, then the country code:
UK – 44
USA and **Canada** – 1
Ireland – 353
Finland – 358

Dial 16115 if you need assistance from an international operator. For direct access to operators abroad, use the following numbers:
AT&T – 80 012 001
MCI – 80 012 122
Canadian Telegraph – 80 012 011
British Telecom – 80 010 441

Internet
Internet cafés in the Old Town include Café el Coctel (Suur-Karja 3) and the smaller Reval Café in the WW Passaž (Aia 3). Nearly every café in central Tallinn offers free WiFi connection for laptop users.

Media
International **newspapers** are sold in major hotels and larger R-Kiosks in central Tallinn. The Apollo bookstore, Viru 23, and the Stockmann department store, Liivalaia 53, offer a decent selection of international magazines. The same vendors sell *The Baltic Times*, an English-language weekly covering news and culture. Of the English-language city guides available, *Tallinn In Your Pocket* is by far the most valuable, with restaurant and pub reviews and masses of practical information.

As far as **television** is concerned, most hotels have satellite or cable hook-ups that bring in international news channels. Estonia only has three television channels, but a lot of entertainment programmes are in English with Estonian subtitles.

Estonian Radio, 103.5MHz FM, rebroadcasts the BBC World Service 7am–8am, 9am–11am, 3pm–7pm and midnight–6am. The same station airs a short bulletin of local news in English on weekdays at 6pm and 7pm.

SPORT

Indoor Swimming Pools
• **Kalev SPA Hotel & Water Park**, Aia 18, tel: 6493 300.
• **Club 26**, Liivalaia 33 (Olümpia Hotel), tel: 6315 585.

Tennis & Squash
• **Coral Club**, Haabersti 5, tel: 6600 520.
• **Pirita Top Tennis**, Regati pst. 1, tel: 6398 836.
• **Metro Squash**, Tondi 17, tel: 6556 392.

Ice Skating
• **Jeti Ice Hall**, Suur-Sõjamäe 14B, tel: 6101 035.
• **Premia Ice Hall**, Haabersi 3, tel: 6600 500.

USEFUL INFORMATION

Travellers with Disabilities
Uneven pavements outside and narrow, medieval staircases inside make exploring the Old Town problematic for anyone in a wheelchair. On the other hand, most of this main area is a pedestrian zone, which means that there is extra room for manoeuvring.

The larger hotels in modern buildings just outside the Old Town have the best wheelchair access; most have specially equipped rooms for disabled guests. Only the newest buildings in Tallinn are ramped. Esra Takso (tel: 1300) provides taxis for disabled passengers.

Children
The most child-friendly way to explore the Old Town is to take a ride on '**Toomas the Train**', a colourful, electric vehicle that makes a non-stop, 20-minute circuit through Tallinn's medieval district. It operates every afternoon (weather permitting) from May to September, departing from Kuninga street, opposite the Olde Hansa restaurant.

Tallinn Zoo (Paldiski mnt. 145; tel: 6943 300), open daily throughout the year, is home to about 350 types of creature. Nearby is the Rocca al Mare Tivoli (Paldiski mnt. 100; tel: 6560 110), where thrilling rides operate from mid-May to August. Older kids can race motorised go-carts or play laser warfare at the **FK Keskus** (Paldiski mnt. 229A; tel: 6870 101; open daily 10am–10pm) at the edge of town.

Museums to look for include the small **Doll Museum** (Kotzebue 16; tel: 6413 941; open Wed–Sun) and the vast, hands-on **Science and Technology Centre** (Põhja pst. 29; tel: 7152 650, open weekdays), known for its weird, interactive displays.

Bookshops

Shops with books in English include Apollo (Viru 23), Rahva Raamat (Viru väljak 4–6, Viru Centre) and Allecto (Juhkentali 8).

Attractions

In terms of tourism, Tallinn is a highly seasonal city. Many outdoor attractions and sightseeing tours operate only in the May–September period. Nearly all museums are closed either on Mondays, Tuesdays or both. In winter, opening hours are usually slightly shorter than in summer. Tickets for adults range from 20–35kr; for children, students and pensioners, they're about 10kr.

The city's **Tallinn Card**, will give you free entrance to all the city's museums and major sights, free sightseeing tours and free use of public transport. It's sold at the Tourist Information Centre and some large hotels. It comes in 24hr (250kr), 48hr (300kr), and 72hr (350kr) varieties.

Language

After Estonian, Russian is the most common first language among locals. Educated Tallinners between the ages of 20 and 40, particularly those in the tourist industry, tend to be very fluent in English. Finnish is also widely understood.

Tourist Information

Tallinn's Tourist Information Centre (www. tourism.tallinn.ee) is at Niguliste 2/Kullassepa 4; tel: 6457 777; open May–June Mon–Fri 9am–7pm, Sat and Sun 10am–5pm; July–Aug Mon–Fri 9am–8pm, Sat and Sun 9am–6pm; Sept Mon–Fri 9am– 6pm, Sat and Sun 10am–5pm; Oct–Apr Mon–Fri 9am–5pm, Sat 10am–3pm. A small branch operates at the Passenger Port's A-Terminal, when ships arrive.

Paid information hotlines such as 1182 and 1188 will give you phone listings and provide a host of useful data including concert and cinema schedules and bus timetables.

Anyone interested in learning more about Estonia will find brochures etc at the Estonia Institute, Suur-Karja 14, tel: 6314 355.

Embassies

Embassy of the Republic of Estonia
16 Hyde Park Gate, London SW7 5DG
Tel: 020 7589 3428; fax: 020 7589 3430
www.estonia.gov.uk
Estonia doesn't have a tourist board in the UK, but the Embassy can help with queries.

FURTHER READING

Insight Guide: Baltic States, Apa Publications. A guide to Estonia, Latvia and Lithuania.
The Devil's Wedding and Other Legends about Tallinn, Perioodika Press. A collection of bizarre folk myths about specific city sights.
The Baltic Revolution, by Anatol Lieven. The definitive work on the Baltic countries' road to independence.
War in the Woods: Estonia's Struggle for Survival 1944–56, by Mart Laar. The heroic story of the 'Forest Brothers', freedom fighters who resisted Soviet occupation.

Above: Tallinn marathon

ACKNOWLEDGEMENTS

Photography and	**Anna Mockford & Nick Bonetti/Apa**
40	**AKG-images London**
59	**Bernard Bisson/Corbis Sygma**
65	**Kaido Haagen/focus.ee**
10	**Lyle Lawson**
29	**Yadid Levy/Alamy**
43T, 43B	**Stanislav Stepaško/KUMU**
1, 2/3, 8/9, 72, 80	**Tallinn City Tourist Office**
73, 88	**The Three Sisters Hotel**
90	**Uniquestay**
52	**Tilt Veermae/Alamy**
60, 61, 62/63	**Gregora Wrona/Apa**
Cover	**Mooch Images/Alamy**

INDEX